The Princess at the Keyboard: Why Girls Should Become Computer Scientists

Amanda J. Stent
Philip M. Lewis
State University of New York
at Stony Brook

http://www.theprincessatthekeyboard.com

First Bytes
The University of Texas at Austin
Department of Computer Science
www.cs.utexas.edu/outreach/first-bytes

The Liberated Queen

With apologies to Joyce Kilmer (1886-1918)

I think that I have never seen
In chess, a liberated queen

A queen who has coequal rights
With all the males like kings and knights

A queen who when she's old and jaded
Isn't sacrificed or traded

In short a queen who'll do her thing
And doesn't have to guard the king

We'll say the queen is liberated
When she and not the king is mated

Chess will have its finest hour
When queens and kings have equal power.

Acknowledgments

We would like to thank Shira Mitchell, a young computer scientist who gave us her picture for the cover of this book. Shira grew up in New York and Tel Aviv. She attended Harvard from 2005 to 2009, studying mathematics and computer science. During this time she explored cryptography, algorithms, and theory of computation. Her interest in randomness in computation inspired her to study probability theory and probabilistic models of evolution. After Harvard, she plans to go to graduate school. She likes computer science because it teaches you to think logically, which is useful in all of science and life in general!

We would also like to thank the other wonderful computer scientists profiled in this book: Maria Klawe, Shafi Goldwasser, Dorothy Denning, Barbara Simons, Jennifer Widom, Marissa Mayer, Sandy Lerner, Daphne Koller, Martha Pollack and Justine Cassell. We were able to contact most of them and they kindly edited their biographies and provided photographs. Any errors in this book are our responsibility, not theirs.

We would like to thank Gustavo Pabon, who provided some of the illustrations for this book: the future computer in Chapter 1, the earring computer in Chapter 2, the stable marriages illustration in Chapter 4 and the voting machine in Chapter 5.

Most of the other illustrations are either created by us or are clipart in the public domain. The illustration of Ada Lovelace in Chapter 1 comes from a painting in the National Physical Gallery, Teddington. The illustration of a punch card was originally printed in the Railroad Gazette, April 19, 1895, and is available from the Library of Congress.

The picture of ENIAC in Chapter 2 comes from ORNL. The picture of Grace Murray Hopper in Chapter 3 comes from the US Navy website. The picture of Deep Blue in Chapter 4 is a snapshot taken in a museum. The photograph of Barbara Simons in Chapter 5 was taken by her husband.

The graph of the number of internet hosts over time in Chapter 7 was created by Ansgar Hellwig and is available from Wikimedia. The picture of a router in this chapter comes from CERN and is available from Wikimedia. The illustration of PageRank was created by Felipe Micaroni Lalli and is available from Wikimedia.

The images from the DARPA Grand Challenges in Chapter 8 come from DARPA (www.darpa.mil). The image of Doug Engelbart's computer interface in Chapter 9 comes from Doug Engelbart. The picture of a Sensable device in this chapter is available from Wikimedia. The picture of an IO Brush is used by permission of Dr. Stephan Marti. The Second Life avatar is Maxval's and is available from Wikimedia.

The graph of CS bachelor's degrees in Chapter 11 comes from the Computing Research Association.

Phil had the idea for this book and kindly invited Amanda to join him in writing it. He also wrote the poem at the front of the book.

Contents

Chapter 1

Why Girls Should Become Computer Scientists

Women have been making important and unique discoveries in computer science since before the first modern computer was built. For example, the very first computer programmer was a woman, Ada Byron Lovelace.

1.1 Ada Lovelace: The First Programmer

Her Life Ada, whose father was the famous poet Lord Byron, was born in England in 1815. Her mother, Annabella Milbanke, left Lord Byron when Ada was one month old, and Ada never saw her father again. In 1835 at the age of 20 Ada married William King, the Earl of Lovelace. They had three children.

As a girl, Ada liked mathematics. Although she could not go to college, she was tutored in mathematics by Mary Somerville, a well-known

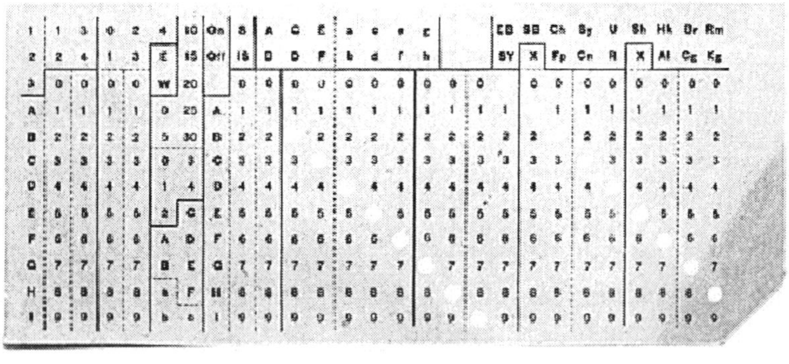

Figure 1.1: A punched card

Name: Ada Byron Lovelace
Born: 1815
Accomplishment: First Programmer

science writer. She later studied more mathematics with Augustus de Moyan at the University of London.

What She Accomplished In 1833 Ada met the mathematician and philosopher Charles Babbage. In 1834, Babbage dreamt up the Analytic Engine, which would have been the first general purpose computer. He planned to build his engine out of mechanical gears and program it with punched cards. The punched cards he wanted to use were used in the textile industry to control the patterns produced by weaving looms.

When Babbage explained the idea of his engine at a dinner party in 1834, Ada was the only guest who understood the importance of his idea. In 1841 another mathematician, Louis Manebrea, presented a paper on Babbage's proposed engine at a conference in Italy. Ada was asked to translate a summary of his talk into English. When she showed Babbage her translation, he asked her to add some notes of her own. The Notes turned out to be twice as long as the summary!

In the Notes Ada made some interesting observations. For example, she said:

> The Analytic Engine ...can do whatever we know how to order it to perform.

That description could still apply to computers today. She also said:

> [the Analytical Engine] might act upon other things besides numbers. ... The engine might compose elaborate and scientific pieces of music of any degree of complexity or extent.

That is an absolutely amazing prediction to have made when computers were only a dream in Babbage's mind and his main goal was to use computers to compute mathematical tables.

> **Sidebar**
>
> Many musicians use computer programs such as MIDI (Musical Instrument Digital Interface). Today there are also several computer programs that make music mostly on their own:
>
> - David Cope's program EMI (Experiments in Musical Intelligence) learns to make music in the style of particular composers.
> - Ben Houge's program Radiospace makes 'random' music by grabbing snippets from the radio.
> - John Biles' program GenJam improvises jazz with a human performer.

Also included in the Notes is the very first computer program: a program to compute a particular mathematical table, the table of Bernoulli numbers. Of course there were no computer languages to write the program in. So Ada first wrote an English language description of how the engine would compute the numbers. Today we would call such a description an *algorithm*. Then she explained how the cards that program the engine should be punched so that the engine would compute the numbers correctly. That description is the first computer program.

The Analytic Engine was never built because of money and other problems, but today's computers are based on the same basic idea. In 1980, the United States Defence Department named a new computer programming language in honor of Ada Lovelace. In 1982 the Association for Women in Computing started awarding an annual Augusta Ada Lovelace Award to a woman who has made "outstanding scientific and technical achievements" in computing.

Stories About Her Ada enjoyed poetry, but her mother did not want her to take after her father. Ada later wrote to her mother, "If you can't give me poetry, can't you give me 'poetical science'?" She also wrote to Charles Babbage, "I do not believe that my father was (or ever could have been) such a Poet as I shall be an Analyst".

To know more about Ada, you can read "Ada, the Enchantress of Numbers" by Betty Toole.

1.2 Why Girls Should Become Computer Scientists

Do you believe that computers can do anything you are smart enough to tell them how to do? What things would you like to tell a computer to do? Perhaps you would like the computer to:

Sidebar

Women are active in using technology to have an impact on society and in politics. Here are two examples:

- At Microsoft, Pam Heath is the lead program coordinator for their Digital Home model. The Digital Home uses a scan of your eye as a virtual door key. It has wall lighting that changes with your mood. Microsoft engineers have created a smart kitchen counter that guesses what you are trying to cook and offers advice. They also exhibit a lamp shade that displays videotaped scenes from your own past.

- Joan Blades, a lawyer and software entrepreneur, is co-founder of MoveOn.org, a political action organization and Web site dedicated to "promoting broad public participation in political discourse."

- Organize your instant messaging chats so you can see your social network;

- Recognize the speech of your teachers so you don't have to take notes in class;

- Manage the fund raising activities of your clubs;

- Let you keep a smart diary or blog in which you combine pictures, words, and music by drag-and-drop

Girls think differently than boys about what kinds of things to do with computers. Read the second quote from Ada's Notes again. While Babbage was interested in using the Analytic Engine to compute mathematical tables, Ada was thinking about using it to compose music. Women today are more likely than men to be interested in using computers to help other people, to change society, and to assist people in their regular lives.

Over your lifetime and beyond, computers will do even more interesting and exciting things – most of which we cannot even imagine now. Some of the revolutionary inventions that have been made just in your lifetime are Google, the iPod, camera phones, instant messaging, YouTube, and Facebook. What will come next? You can help make it happen. We need as many different perspectives as possible to think about what these things should be and then how to implement them.

So, one reason girls should become computer scientists is that society needs women to bring their unique perspective to the field. But there is another important reason: it's fun! Yes, there are limitations on what computers can do. That is one of the important aspects of computer science that we will discuss in this book. But when you are writing a program for a computer, you don't feel that way. You feel that the computer can do anything – limited only by your skills and creativity.

Figure 1.2: *Not the computer of the future!*

Of course, you have to devote some time and effort to learn about computer science. But when you use your computing knowledge to program the computer to do something new and exciting, that effort will be worth it. Computer science gives you the opportunity to use your imagination and creativity to think of and build something completely new, that will change your life and the lives of others.

Our goal in this book is to make you excited about computer science, perhaps so excited that you decide to become a computer scientist.

Chapter 2

What Is Computer Science All About?

2.1 What is a Computer?

Computers are everywhere. You probably have many of them in your house – not only in your PC, but also in your cell phone, your iPod, your cable box, your parents' car, and maybe even your watch. In fact, there are probably many more computers living in your house than people.

Over the years, computers have been built using many different components: mechanical gears, electrical switches, relays, vacuum tubes, transistors, integrated circuits – and who knows what they will be built out of next. So just what is a computer?

That question is not so easy to answer. Until after World War II, the word "computer" referred to a person. Many people, particularly young women, were employed as computers. The First Edition of the Oxford English Dictionary (1928) defined a computer as

> One who computes, a calculator, reckoner: specifically, a person employed to make calculations in an observatory, in surveying, etc.

Now, more than half a century later in the "computer age," computers are devices that come in all sizes and shapes. One informal definition would be a simple expansion of Ada Lovelace's observation:

> A computer is a device that does exactly what you instruct it to do.

Notice that we used the words "instruct it to do," not the words "tell it to do." You cannot just tell a computer what to do; you have to give it detailed step-by-step instructions on how to do it. As with Ada Lovelace's description, the instructions might first be an English language description, called an *algorithm*. Or they might be in some computer language, called a *program*. We talk more about algorithms and programs later.

Figure 2.1: *ENIAC: The first general purpose digital computer (1945). ENIAC was programmed mostly by women, including Kay Antonelli, Jean Bartik, Betty Holberton, Marlyn Meltzer, Frances Spence, and Ruth Teitelbaum. Someone said that Betty Holberton "could do more logical reasoning while she was asleep than most people can do awake."*

Our definition of a computer can also be applied to the people who had jobs as "computers" except that the instructions given to the people probably did not have to be as detailed as those given to a computing device. So it doesn't make any difference what a computer is made of. It might be made of mechanical gears, vacuum tubes, transistors, integrated circuits, or some other material. The important thing is that a computer does whatever you instruct it to do. The details about how to "instruct" a computer to do things, and the types of things that you can "instruct" a computer to do, are the basis for all the interesting computer science questions about how computers behave.

2.2   What is Computer Science?

What is computer science? First of all, computer science is not about how many gigabytes you should have on your hard disk, or how fast a connection you should have to the internet. And it is not about just programming. It is much more basic than that.

Computer science is about the answers to two questions:

1. What are the limitations on what computers can do? The answers to such questions are studied in **Theoretical Computer Science**.

2. How can we make computers do new and exciting things (within those limitations)? The answers to such questions are studied in **Experimental Computer Science**.

2.2.1 Theoretical Computer Science

You might think that since a computer can do anything you instruct it to do, there are no limitations on what a computer can do. Not true! There are two kinds of limitations.

How Long It Takes One limitation is on the speed at which the computer can carry out your instructions. Let's start with a simple example that at first doesn't even seem related to computer science. Say a bad guy wants to break into your school locker, but you have a digital combination lock. One thing the bad guy might do is to try all possible combinations on your lock until he finds the one that works. There might be as many as 100,000 possible combinations, so that would take a long time. But a computer could try all 100,000 possible combinations before you could blink your eyes. However, suppose you had a lock with

$$10,000,000,000,000,000,000,000,000,000,000$$

possible combinations. Now if the bad guy asked a computer to try all possible combinations, it would take it a very very long time. Suppose a very fast computer could try a million different combinations a second. It would take it more than a trillion trillion years to try all the possible combinations. A trillion trillion looks like this:

$$1,000,000,000,000,000,000,000,000$$

But a trillion trillion years is much longer than the age of the universe, which is "only" about 14 billion years. 14 billion looks like this:

$$14,000,000,000$$

Therefore the computer obviously can't use this method to break into your locker. Even if the computer were a million times faster and could try a million million possible combinations a second, it still could not use this method. The universe would most likely end first.

Of course there are no combination locks that have this many possible combinations. But the same reasoning applies in a different, very practical situation that is related to computer science. When you buy something over the internet and send your credit card number to the merchant, that credit card number is written in code, or *encrypted*, and then sent as a message over the internet. The merchant's computer decodes, or decrypts, the message using a decryption key similar to the combination on a combination lock. However, the number of possible decryption keys in the internet system is more than

$$10,000,000,000,000,000,000,000,000,000,000$$

Sidebar

In some respects a computer is like Aladdin's magic genie, who would do whatever Aladdin wanted it to do. But there is an important difference. Aladdin's genie did *whatever Aladdin wanted it to do*, while a computer does *whatever you give it detailed instructions to do*. Suppose you want to build a new castle. Aladdin's magic genie would build the castle instantly, but your computer might take a very long time to carry out the instructions you gave it. Also, Aladdin's magic genie would build exactly the castle Aladdin wanted. But if the instructions you give your computer are not exactly correct, the castle might end up looking more like a diner than a castle, or it might just collapse in a big heap.

If a bad guy wants to steal your credit card number he has to steal the encrypted message and decrypt it. But if he writes a computer program to try all possible decryption keys, that computer program would require more time than the age of the universe to complete.

Decrypting a message without knowing the decryption key is called **breaking the encryption system**. One way to break an encryption system is to try all possible decryption keys. You might think that maybe there is some other, faster method the bad guy could use. But it turns out that there is no method known that is significantly faster than trying all possible keys. All of which should make us feel pretty safe about buying things over the internet.

In this example, we can give a computer a simple set of instructions (try all possible decryption keys, one at a time), but it would take the computer an impossibly long amount of time to complete those instructions. As we shall see in Chapter 4, there are some problems that can be done in a short time, other problems that take a longer amount of time, and some problems, like this one, that take an impossibly long time. The part of computer science that deals with how long it takes a computer to solve problems is called **computational complexity**.

What Can and Cannot be Done   There are some tasks that are simple to describe, but that cannot be described as instructions to a computer. A computer just cannot do these tasks.

Suppose we have a computer program that runs on Windows, and we want to rewrite it so that it runs on OS X. When we are done, we would like to know if the rewritten program is **equivalent** to the original one; that is, if it produces the same output for all inputs. It would be nice if we could instruct a computer how to examine any two computer programs and say whether or not they produce the same output for all possible inputs. Such a program would be very useful to Microsoft and Apple, as well as all the other software companies. They could develop programs that are more reliable, and that would make us all happy.

Unfortunately, such a set of instructions does not exist. Determining

---

Sidebar

To see how fast things have changed in computer science and how difficult it is to predict future changes, read the following quotes from famous people and organizations:

I think there is a world market for maybe five computers.
Thomas Watson, Chairman of IBM: 1943

Computers in the future may weigh no more than 1.5 tons.
Popular Mechanics: 1949

There is no reason anyone would want a computer in their home.
Ken Olson, founder of Digital Equipment Corporation: 1977

640K (of memory) ought to be enough for anybody. (Today's PCs have more than 1000 times that much memory).
Bill Gates, founder of Microsoft: 1981

---

whether two programs are equivalent is an example of a problem that is said to be **non-computable**. It cannot be done by any computer – past, present, or future – no matter what components it is built from, how big it is, how powerful it is, how fast it goes, how much memory it has, or how long we are willing to wait for it to finish. And that's bad news for people who build programs and for people who use them.

Interestingly, if a problem is non-computable so that there is no set of instructions you can give a computer to do that problem, there is no set of instructions you can give to a person to do that problem either.

We will learn more about theoretical computer science in Chapter 4.

2.2.2 Experimental Computer Science

Experimental computer science is about making computers do new and exciting things. So why are there always so many new and exciting things that computers can do? Every year there seems to be at least one new computer-based device or application that we become addicted to and just have to have.

In 1965 Gordon Moore, founder of the Intel chip manufacturing company, made the predication that

> *The number of transistors that can be put on a computer chip will double every 18 months.*

This prediction is now called **Moore's Law**, and research at chip-making companies has kept that "law" true ever since then. It appears that Moore's Law will remain true for the foreseeable future.

When the number of transistors on a chip doubles, the computers you can build with those chips are half the size and compute twice as

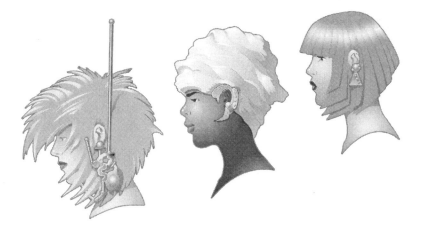

Figure 2.2: *What an earring computer might look like.*

fast. Applications that were not practical to build all of a sudden become practical. For example, the first commercial camera phone was introduced in 2000. It would not have been possible to put a camera in a cell phone just a few years before that. Today's cell phones are often half the size of pre-2000 cell phones, but most of them have cameras!

Over the past 40 years, this decrease in computer size and increase in computer speed has had a profound effect on computer science and on society. What will happen ten years from now? Probably computers that are many times more powerful than today's PCs will be small enough, say, to fit into an earring. What things could such a computer do?

Suppose you predicted that earring computers would be useful as language translators. When you visited a foreign country, say China, the earring would automatically translate Chinese into English and whisper that translation directly into your ear. If you were a computer scientist today, you might start working on programs that would perform such language translation. You might perform your research on large desktop computers. But you would be confident that in a few years, your programs would fit into an earring computer.

Much of the best work in computer science is both theoretical and experimental. For example, Ron Rivest, Adi Shamir, and Leonard Adleman invented the internet encryption system at MIT in 1997. They first developed the theory showing that decrypting a message without the decryption key is very hard for a computer to do, which was theoretical computer science. Then they built and demonstrated the system, which was experimental computer science. (Then they formed a company to market the technology and got rich, which is another interesting possibility in computer science.)

Sidebar

Some historical facts about "firsts" in computer science:

- The first use of the term "computer science" was in 1957 by Louis Fein, who recommended that Stanford establish a Graduate School of Computer Science. The first published use of the term was in Fein's 1959 paper, *The Role of the University in Computers, Data Processing, and Related Fields.*

- The first Computer Science Department was established in 1962 at Purdue University. Stanford's CS department was founded in 1965 and Stony Brook's in 1969.

- The first computer science textbook was published in 1969, and the first author was a women. The book was A.I. Forsythe, T.A. Keenan, E.I. Organick, and W. Stenberg, *Computer Science: A First Course*, published by Wilcy & Sons.

- The first use of the term "software" was in 1958 by John Tukey, a statistician at Princeton University and Bell Laboratories, in an article entitled *The Teaching of Concrete Mathematics* that appeared in the *American Mathematical Monthly*.

- The first published use of the term "bit" (standing for binary digit, which can be either 1 or 0) was in 1948 by Claude Shannon, a mathematician at Bell Laboratories, in the classic paper *A Mathematical Theory of Communication*. But interestingly, in that paper Shannon says John Tukey invented the term "bit". Tukey remembered that the term evolved over a lunch table conversation in 1943.

- The first use of the term "byte" (which means 8 bits and can be used to store one character) was in 1956 by Werner Bucholoz during the design of the IBM Stretch computer.

2.3 What Is A Computer Scientist?

Undergraduate and graduate degrees in computer science are all professional degrees. A computer scientist is a professional who has specialized knowledge and expertise about computer software and hardware, including: operating systems, computer networks, databases, programming languages, software engineering, computer graphics, computer architecture, artificial intelligence, and human-computer interaction. You can see from this list that computer science is about a lot more than just computer programming.

Computer scientists can work for computer software or hardware companies, banks, insurance companies, stock brokers, manufacturing companies, internet companies, start-up companies, entertainment and music companies, movie studios, defense contractors, biotech companies, universities, hospitals, and the government.

Some of the job titles they can have (in addition to computer scientist) are: software engineer, computer programmer, Web programmer, game programmer, systems analyst, consultant, network engineer, usability engineer, systems administrator, project or program manager, corporate manager, college professor, and researcher.

2.4   What Do Computer Scientists Do All Day?

What do computer scientists do all day? You might have heard that all they do is sit by themselves at a computer terminal, eat pizza, drink soft drinks, and type away. There might be some computer scientists who actually do that. But most computer scientists spend most of their time interacting with other people.

For example, suppose you were interested in making an earring computer that could translate from one language to another. You might first read technical papers written by other people who are working on language translation. Then you might talk with some linguists to discuss the structure of languages and how they might be translated. You might also develop your ideas with other computer scientists. You might write some programs to try out your ideas and make some experiments translating some real people speaking. Based on the results of these experiments you might refine your programs and try some more experiments. When your work had reached an appropriate stage, you might present it at a technical conference, where you would meet people from all over the world working on this or related problems. And who knows – you might even get famous (or rich if you start a company to market your ideas).

We talk more about this in Chapter 11.

2.5   Maria Klawe: First Woman To Serve as Dean of Engineering at Princeton

In addition to being the first women to serve as Dean of the School of Engineering and Applied Science at Princeton University, Maria Klawe is a watercolor artist, a runner, a kayaker, an electric guitarist, and a mother. Her latest passion is learning to ride a skate-board.

Her Life   Maria was born in Toronto, Canada in 1951. She received her B.Sc. (1973) and Ph.D (1977) in mathematics from the University of Alberta. She remembers the faculty saying when she was an undergraduate that "you'll never stay in math."

She became interested in computer science and, in 1978, joined the Computer Science Department at the University of Toronto, first as a graduate student, and then as an Assistant Professor.

Name: Maria Klawe
Born: 1951
Accomplishment: First Woman Dean of Engineering at Princeton

In 1980 she married Nick Pippenger, a theoretical computer scientist, and they moved to California to join the theory group at what is now the IBM Almaden Research Center. While at IBM Maria had two children, a boy named Janek, and a girl named Sasha.

In 1988 Maria and Nick joined the University of British Columbia, where Maria served as Head of the Department of Computer Science from 1988 to 1995, Vice-President of Student and Academic Services from 1995 to 1998, and Dean of Science from 1998 to 2002. When UBC invited first year students to a Meet the Dean event in 2002, Maria surprised the students by playing some classics on her guitar.

In 2003 Maria and Nick moved to Princeton, where Maria was the Dean of the School of Engineering and Applied Science.

In 2006 Maria and Nick moved back to California, where Maria is currently the President of Harvey Mudd College, a science-based university in Claremont, California.

What She Accomplished   Over the years, Maria's research has been mainly in theoretical computer science, mathematics, and the interaction between computer science and mathematics.

Maria is interested in how computers can be used to teach middle school and high school school students mathematics and computer science. She was the founder and director of the EGEMS project (Electronic Games for Education in Mathematics and Science), which made mathematics games for students in grades 4 to 9. Research done by EGEMS also identified significant differences in how boys and girls interact with computers and software.

Maria has received many awards and held many leadership positions in professional organizations both in the United States and Canada. From 2002 to 2004, she served as President of the Association for Computing Machinery (ACM), the professional society for computer scientists and other computing professionals. She was the fourth women to serve as President of the ACM since it was founded in 1947. The other three were Jean Sammet (1974-1976), Adele Goldberg (1984-1986), and Barbara Simons (1988-2000). She served as Chair of the Board of the Anita Borg Institute for Women and Technology from 2003 to 2008.

Stories About Her   At the 2005 Microsoft Research Summit, Maria had a public discussion with Bill Gates about the problem of attracting more high school students, especially girls, to become computer scientists. The discussion began with the following exchange:

Maria Klawe: So this morning Bill, I'd like to start off with a really important question. How many of the Harry Potter books have you read so far?

Bill Gates: Well it's a phenomenon that I'm going to have to get myself more immersed in. I read two and then my daughter decided they were a little too scary. But now I understand that even adults are supposed to read them. In fact, I'm curious what do you think is going to happen, what would you like to see happen in the Harry Potter series?

Maria Klawe: Well I have one special dream and I'd love to see Hermione choose to become a computer scientist. I think that would really turn around our problem, especially for young girls.

Chapter 3

Programs and Compilers

3.1 What is a Program?

We said that a computer will do anything you instruct it to do. So how do you give it instructions? We might start the same way that Ada Lovelace did in her Notes, by writing a simple English language description of what we want the computer to do – an algorithm.

Let's consider a very simple problem: giving a grade for a test. An algorithm for what we want to do is:

1. *Input the test score*

2. *If the test score is greater than 65, give the student a grade of P, meaning that she has passed; otherwise give the student a grade of F, meaning that she has failed.*

3. *Output the grade.*

Now we will use this algorithm as a guide to write a **program** in a **programming language**. A programming language is made up of **statements**. One statement that we use in our program is

```
if (testScore > 65) {grade = 'P'} else {grade = 'F'}
```

which means that if the score on the test is greater than 65, the grade for the test is P (the student passed). Otherwise the grade is F (the student failed).

This statement is called an *if statement*. The statement first checks the *condition* inside the parentheses ( ) after the `if`. If the condition is true, it does the statement (or statements) inside the braces { } after the condition. If the condition is false, it does the statement(s) inside the braces after the `else`.

Figure 3.1: *A web browser is a program with if and while statements. What other programs do you use?*

This *if* statement is simple enough that a human can understand it and exact enough that a computer can understand it. Such *if* statements are the way the computer makes decisions. In this example, it is a translation of the second step in our algorithm from English into a programming language.

To carry out the algorithm we need to add two additional *input/output statements*, one to input the test score and one to output the grade.

```
input(testScore)
if (testScore > 65) {grade = 'P'} else {grade = 'F'}
output(grade)
```

The statements inside the braces:

```
grade = 'P'
```

and

```
grade = 'F'
```

are called *assignment statements* because they assign the values 'P' and 'F' to grade. We can think of testScore and grade as pieces of paper with labels on them, where the computer can keep track of what it has to know.

Our program is almost complete. We just have to add two additional statements, called *declarations*, to tell the computer that testScore is an integer (a whole number) and grade is a character (a letter).

```
integer testScore
character grade
input(testScore)
if (testScore > 65) {grade = 'P'} else {grade = 'F'}
output(grade)
```

Now the program is complete.

Sidebar

Try your hand at writing a program using a `while` statement that inputs a number n and outputs the value of n factorial (written $n!$), where :

$$n! = n * (n - 1) * (n - 2) * ... * 3 * 2 * 1.$$

For example:

$$5! = 5 * 4 * 3 * 2 * 1 = 120$$

The While Statement You might think that the simple statements in this program come from a "toy" computer language that has no relation to the real world. In fact, they are not part of any real computer language. However, if we add just one more statement type to our toy language, it would be completely general. Any application we can program in any real computer language, we could program in our toy language. That new statement type is the `while` statement.

As we shall see, a `while` statement repeats a sequence of statements over and over again as long as (while) some condition is true. The `while` statement is easy to understand, but is the cause of most of the complications (and fun) in programming. A simple example of a program using a `while` statement is:

```
integer testNumber
input(testNumber)
while (testNumber > 0)
    {output(testNumber)
    testNumber = testNumber - 1}
```

The program first inputs an integer into `testNumber`; say it inputs the number 2. Then it gets to the `while` statement. The `while` statement consists of the line following the word `while` and the following two indented lines within the braces, { }:

```
while (testNumber > 0)
    {output(testNumber)
    testNumber = testNumber - 1}
```

The `while` statement first checks the condition inside the parentheses ( ) after the `while`. If the condition is false, the `while` statement completes and does not do the statements inside the braces. If the condition is true, it does the statements inside the braces and then "loops back" and starts running all over again. (The `while` statement is sometimes called a while loop.)

In our example, the condition is true because `testNumber` is equal to 2 and 2 is greater than 0. Therefore the `while` statement does the two

---

Sidebar

What does the following program do?

```
integer newNumber
newNumber = 1
while (newNumber > 0)
   {newNumber = 2}
```

When the program enters the `while` loop the first time, the condition, `(newNumber > 0)`, is true because `newNumber` equals 1. So the program executes the statement in the loop and loops back to execute the loop again. Then, since the statement in the loop made `newNumber` equal to 2, the condition is true the second time the program enters the loop. In fact the condition is true *every time* around the loop. We say the program is **stuck in a loop**. All the user sees is that the program never stops. The computer on which it is executing just seems frozen. You have probably seen this happen with programs on your own computer.

You might think the person who wrote the program could easily determine whether or not the program would ever get stuck in a loop. That is certainly true for this simple program, but might not be true for a more complicated program, perhaps containing thousands of different statements with many while loops. Since we have all seen examples of programs that get stuck in a loop, it is obviously quite hard to make sure that a program will not get stuck in a loop.

It would be nice if we could write a program to tell us if another program will get stuck in a loop. Unfortunately, determining whether a program will ever get caught in a loop is a non-computable problem (Section 2.2.1).

---

statements inside the braces. It first outputs a 2. Then it gets to the assignment statement:

```
testNumber = testNumber - 1
```

You might ask, how can `testNumber` be equal to `testNumber - 1`? One way to think about it is to imagine that the computer is going to cross out the number it has written on the piece of paper labeled `testNumber` and write down that number minus 1 instead. So in our example, it will cross out '2' and write down '1'.

After going through the statements inside the braces, the `while` statement "loops back" and starts running all over again.

In our example, it again checks the condition inside the parentheses and since `testNumber` now equals 1, and 1 is greater than 0, the condition is again true and it again does the two statements inside the braces. It outputs 1 and then sets `testNumber` to 0.

This time when the `while` statement loops back and starts running all over again, the condition inside the parentheses is false, since `testNumber` equals 0, and 0 is not greater than 0. Because the condition is false, the `while` statement does not do the statements inside the braces. In fact, since there are no more statements in the program, the program finishes. The program has output:

2, 1

If, instead of 2, we had input 6, it would have output:

6, 5, 4, 3, 2, 1

If we had input 1,000,000, it would have output:

1,000,000, 999,999, 999,998, ... , 3, 2, 1

Of course it would take a long time to output all of those numbers. This is an example where a very short program can take a very long time to execute (because the `while` statement goes around its loop many times). That is one of the interesting possible behaviors of `while` statements.

Remember the program from Section 2.2.1 that attempts to break the internet encryption system by trying all possible decryption keys? That program takes a very long time to execute because it goes around a `while` loop many many times as it tries all possible decryption keys one at a time.

You can try your hand at programming with a `while` statement using the example in the first Sidebar. You can explore another interesting possible behavior of `while` statements in the second Sidebar.

These sample statements do not come from any real programming language. However, real programming languages do have statements that are very similar to these statements – for example some kind of *if* statement, some kind of *while* statement, some kind of *assignment* statement, some input/output statements, and some declarations. If you want to learn more about how to program, a good place to start is http://www.alice.org.

3.2 What is a Compiler?

When we wrote our first program, we translated our algorithm from English into a programming language. Before a computer can execute the program, it must be translated again, from a programming language into the language used by a particular computer's hardware, the **machine language**. A program called a **compiler** performs this translation.

You know, of course, that there are different types of computers available today, such as PCs and Apples. You might also have heard of some of the programming languages in use today; Java, C++, Fortran, Cobol,

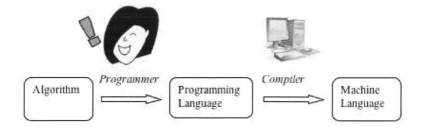

Figure 3.2: *Going from an algorithm to a programming language to the machine language of a specific computer*

etc. There must be a different compiler to translate programs written in each of these programming languages into the machine language of each type of computer. So there must be a compiler that translates programs written in C++ into the machine language of the PC, and there must be a different compiler to translate programs written in C++ into the machine language of the Apple. And so on.

One advantage of using compilers is that the same program written in some programming language, for example C++, can be run on many different computers – in fact any computer for which there is a compiler for that language. Before compilers were invented, programs had to be written directly in the machine language of the specific computer on which they would run, and so could run only on that computer. This made a lot of work for computer scientists, and meant that good programs could not be used as much as people wanted. So, the invention of the compiler was an important event in computer science.

3.3   Grace Murray Hopper: Inventor of the First Compiler

The very first compiler was invented by a woman: Grace Murray Hopper.

Her Life   Grace Brewster Murray was born in 1906. She was interested in mathematics and engineering from the time she was a child. There is a story that when she was seven years old, she took apart seven clocks she found in her house to find out how they worked!

In 1928, Grace graduated from Vassar College with a bachelor's degree in Mathematics and Physics. In 1934 she was the first woman to receive a Ph.D. in Mathematics from Yale University. She started teaching Mathematics at Vassar in 1931.

Grace married Vincent Foster Hopper in 1930, but he died during World War II.

Name: Grace Murray Hopper
Born: 1906
Accomplishment: Inventor of First Compiler

What She Accomplished   When World War II started, Grace joined the United States Naval Reserves as a lieutenant, where she was assigned to the Bureau of Ordinance Computation Project at Harvard University. She learned to program one of the first general-purpose computers ever built, the Mark I electromechanical computer. She programmed this computer using machine language.

In 1949, when the war was over, Grace joined the Eckert-Mauchly Computer Corporation (which later became Remington Rand) as a senior mathematician. In 1967 she rejoined the Navy where she later retired as a Rear Admiral.

In 1952 Remington Rand produced Univac, the first commercial computer (made from vacuum tubes). That same year, Grace developed the first compiler, the A-0 compiler, which ran on the Univac. In 1956, she developed a compiler called B-0 or Flow-Matic, for business applications. When we say that Grace developed a compiler called Flow-Matic, we mean that she developed a programming language called Flow-Matic and a compiler that translated that language into the machine language of the Univac.

Flow-Matic had a significant influence on the development of COBOL (Common Business Oriented Language), which was developed in 1959 by a committee organized by the U.S. Department of Defense. Grace Hopper was one of the two technical advisors to that committee. COBOL is still in use today, and is probably the most widely used computer language in the world.

Among the many honors awarded to Grace Murray Hopper were the National Medal of Technology and the Department of Defense Distinguished Service Medal. She became the first person from the United States and the first woman from any country to be made a Distinguished Fellow of the British Computer Society. She has had a guided missile destroyer, the USS Hopper, named after her. In 1983 she was awarded the Augusta Ada Lovelace Award by the Association for Women in Computing.

Stories About Her   During her lifetime Grace was known as "Grand Lady Software," "Amazing Grace." and "Grandma Cobol." While she was working at Harvard, a moth was found in one of the relays in the computer that caused it to work incorrectly. When the moth was removed, she said they were "debugging the system." Thus the term *computer bug* is often attributed to her. The moth was taped to her logbook, which is now the property of the Smithsonian Institute.

While Grace was working at Eckert-Mauchly, she said she liked hiring women because

> *Women turn out to be very good programmers for one very good reason. They tend to finish up things and men don't very often finish.*

Chapter 4

Algorithms

4.1 What is an Algorithm?

In Chapters 1 and 3 we said that an algorithm is a human-language description of the instructions we give a computer to tell it how to do something. Computer scientists spend a lot of time thinking about algorithms. In this chapter we will give some examples of algorithms. But before we do that, we have to say exactly what an algorithm is.

> An algorithm for a problem is a step-by-step procedure for solving that problem that is guaranteed to eventually complete and produce the correct answer to that problem. An algorithm has one or more inputs and produces one or more outputs.

Actually, you have already learned many algorithms. In elementary school you learned simple algorithms for performing arithmetic. For example, you learned an algorithm for multiplying two large numbers, say 728 and 345. The algorithm has several basic steps, including: multiplying two single digit numbers, adding two single digit numbers, and the carry operation in adding columns of numbers. You didn't think of it as an algorithm when you learned it in third grade, but that's what it is.

You also probably know algorithms for adding a new number to your cell phone, uploading a picture to your blog, or using a vending machine. Even a shampoo bottle has an algorithm on it: *Wash, Rinse, Repeat!*

The concept of an algorithm is one of the most important ideas in computer science. Once we have an algorithm for a problem, we can write a program corresponding to that algorithm in any computer language to run on any computer. We can also analyze the algorithm to determine how much time it requires to complete. We will give examples of such analyses later in this chapter.

4.1.1   Example Algorithm: Searching a Phone Book

Suppose you are interested in searching your cell phone's contact list to
find the phone number of your friend, and the contact list contains 1024
names. (You will see why we picked that exact number of names a little
later.) One simple algorithm for performing the search is:

1. Start at the beginning of the contact list and look at all the names,
   one at a time, until you find the name you are looking for.

2. If you find the name you are looking for, stop and report the phone
   number for that name.

3. If you get to the end of the contact list and have not yet found the
   name, stop and report that the name is not in the list.

This algorithm is called the **linear search algorithm** because it searches
all the names in the contact list, one at a time, in order.

Now that we have seen this algorithm, we can be more specific about
the definition of "algorithm". Each step in an algorithm must be a simple
operation that can be easily done in a short amount of time. So one step
in an algorithm for searching a contact list cannot be

Search the contact list to see if the desired name is in it.

but can be

See if the next name in the contact list is the name you want.

If the problem can have more than one possible input, the algorithm
must give the right answer for all the possible inputs. For example, the
contact list searching problem has two inputs: a contact list and a name
to search for. There are many possible contact lists and many possible
names. An algorithm for contact list searching must produce the correct
answer for all possible contact lists and all possible names.

As we have said, once we have an algorithm for a problem, we can
analyze how many steps are required to carry out that algorithm. The
time required to complete the linear search algorithm depends on where
the name is in the contact list. If the name begins with A, the search will
be short. If it begins with Z, it will be long.

When we analyze an algorithm to figure out how long it takes to run,
we usually determine the **worst-case time**. For different inputs, the
algorithm might execute a different number of steps and take a different
amount of time. What is the longest time it can ever take? For the linear
search algorithm, the worst case is when the name we want is the last
name in the contact list (or is not in the contact list at all), and, in our
example, the algorithm has to examine all 1024 names in the contact list
to find it. To search for a particular name in a contact list of n names
using the linear search algorithm, we would have to look at n names in
the worst case. We say that the **complexity** of this algorithm is n (the
number of names it looks at).

Sidebar

Some places in your house are full of algorithms. For example, go into your bathroom and look on the back of the bottles and jars in the medicine cabinet. How many algorithms can you find?

Where else in your house might there be lots of algorithms?

We especially want to know the **worst-case behavior** for algorithms because it gives us a guarantee that the algorithm will never take a longer time. For many algorithms the worst case (or something close to it) happens fairly often.

The linear search algorithm seems inefficient. If you were searching for a name in the contact list, you certainly wouldn't use that algorithm! Say you were looking up Sarah Silver. You would probably scroll down the contact list to about two thirds of the way through and see what letters the name on that screen began with. If they did not begin with 'S', you would estimate how much further down to scroll. And so on.

Let's see if we can create an algorithm that is closer to what you would do. This algorithm is called the **binary search algorithm**. As we will see, the worst case for the binary search algorithm occurs when the name being searched for is the last name in the contact list *and* when the name being searched for is the first name in the contact list. So let's assume we are searching for the first name, say **Alice Aaron**.

1. Start by looking at the middle name in the contact list, the 512th name.

2. If that is the name you are looking for, stop and report the phone number of that name.

3. If it is not the name you are looking for, you at least know which half of the contact list the name is in (because the names are in alphabetic order). Suppose the middle name is **Mary Middleton**.

4. Since you are looking for **Aaron**, you know that it is earlier in the alphabet than **Middleton**, so you know it is in the first half of the contact list.

5. Repeat this plan on the first half of the contact list. Look at the middle name in the first half of the contact list, the 256th name.

6. If that is the name you are looking for, stop and report the phone number of that name.

7. If it is not the name you are looking for, you now know which quarter of the contact list the name is in.

8. And so you repeat the whole plan again.

In the worst case, where the name you are looking for is the first name in the contact list, Aaron, you would look at the

512th name

256th name

128th name

64th name

32th name

16th name

8th name

4th name

2nd name

1st name

and you would find the name by looking at 10 names.

Of course this particular worst case is where the desired name is the first name in the contact list, and you would have found that name right away with the linear search algorithm. But the binary search algorithm would always find the name by looking at no more than 10 names, even if the desired name were the last in the contact list, where the linear search algorithm would have looked at 1024 names.

The gain using the binary search algorithm is even more for larger contact lists. If the contact list were twice as large (2048 entries), the linear search algorithm would take twice as long because it might have to examine 2048 names. But the binary search algorithm would have to examine only one more name, for a total of 11. It would first look at the 1024th name, and if that is not the name it was looking for, it would know which half of the contact list the name is in and would use the above method on those 1024 names.

To see how this works for contact lists with different numbers of names, suppose the contact list had

1 name, it would look at that 1 name

2 names, it would look at a maximum of 2 names

8 names, it would look at a maximum of 3 names

....

1,024 names, it would look at a maximum of 10 names

....

1,048,576 names, it would look at a maximum of 20 names

As you can see, these numbers increase very slowly as the number of names in the contact list increases. The last item on the list is amazing. Even if the contact list has a million names in it, the algorithm never looks at more than 20 names. If there were a phone book for the entire

---

Sidebar

Trick Question – the Index Search Algorithm: Suppose the phone book has an index so that, for example, if the you wanted to look up **Jane Jones** in the contact list, the *index search algorithm* could immediately find the first name in the contact list that begins with the letter **J**. Then the algorithm looks at all the names beginning with **J**, one at a time, looking for **Jane Jones**. Suppose the contact list has n names. How many names would the *index search algorithm* have to look at in the worst case? Remember this is a trick question. Think about the problem for a few minutes before reading the answer.

Answer: The worst case occurs when all the n names in the contact list begin with **J** and **Jane Jones** is the last name in the list of **J** names. In the worst case, the algorithm would have to look at n names.

Of course, in the real world it is very unlikely that this worst case situation would ever occur. An index is usually a big help in searching.

---

population of the United States, we could search for a name in that book by looking at no more than 28 names.

In the general case, if we are given a list of n names, the number of names we would have to look at is equal to the number of times we must divide n by 2 until we get to 1. Mathematicians have a notation for the number of times you must divide a number n by 2 before you get 1. They call it logarithm to the base 2 of n, which they write as $log_2(n)$. An equivalent way to think about $log_2(n)$ is the number of times 2 has to be multiplied by itself to get n. So, for example $log_2(1024)$ equals 10 because

$$1024 = 2 * 2 * 2 * 2 * 2 * 2 * 2 * 2 * 2 * 2$$

You might be more familiar with the logarithms you are studying in school, logarithms to the base 10, written as $log_{10}(n)$, and sometimes just as $log(n)$, which is the number of times n can be divided by 10 before you get 1. For example $log(1000)$ equals 3.

So to search for a particular name in a list of n names using the binary search algorithm, we would have to look at $log_2(n)$ names in the worst case. In all the examples we give, $log_2(n)$ is an integer, but in case it is not, for example if n is 1030, then we would have to split the list in half one more time and we would need to look at 11 names.

We have seen two algorithms for the searching problem, one that has a complexity of n and one that has a complexity of $log_2(n)$. It can be proved that there is no algorithm for the searching problem with a complexity of less than $log_2(n)$. Therefore we say than the complexity of the searching *problem* is $log_2(n)$. The complexity of a problem is the complexity of the fastest algorithm for that problem. Because the complexity of the searching problem increases so slowly as n increases, we say that the searching problem is **easy**.

Figure 4.1: *Will this marriage be stable?*

Some computer scientists spend their careers developing efficient algorithms and publishing these algorithms in papers and books, and sometimes writing programs for these algorithms in popular computer languages. Often they post their algorithms and programs on the internet and make them available to be downloaded for free.

Other computer scientists and computer professionals learn these algorithms in school, read these books and papers, and keep abreast of what is available over the internet, so they can use these algorithms and programs in the programs they are writing.

4.1.2   Example Algorithm: The Stable Marriage Problem

We now discuss a problem that is also easy, but is a bit more fun: the stable marriage problem. Suppose we have n men and n women who want to get married. Each of the women prepares a list of the n men ordered by her preference, and each of the men prepares a similar list of the n women ordered by his preference. The problem is to match up the men and women so that they all have happy marriages.

Of course no man or woman is guaranteed to get his or her first choice. But we want to guarantee that all marriages are *stable*. By that we mean that the following situation cannot occur.

Sarah is married to Sam.

Janet is married to John.

But in the rankings,

Sarah prefers John to Sam.

John prefers Sarah to Janet.

In this case, Sarah and John would divorce their spouses, run away, and get married.

The question is, can we find an algorithm that produces marriages in which this situation does not occur, so that we can say the marriages are stable?

You might think that this problem is silly. But this is exactly the problem faced every year by new doctors in picking the hospitals at which they will do their residencies. The residents rank the hospitals, and the hospitals rank the residents. Then a stable marriage algorithm is used to assign residents to hospitals. In 2008 the algorithm was used to assign more than 23,000 new doctors to their residencies. The assignments are performed by the National Resident Matching Program, a nonprofit organization.

Here is an algorithm that solves the stable marriage problem for n men and n women and has a complexity of n^2. (This problem is harder than the searching problem, but still certainly doable by a computer.) The algorithm proceeds in rounds.

1. In round 1, each man proposes to the woman who he loves the most (who is first on his list).

   (a) If a woman has not yet been proposed to and gets a proposal, she accepts that proposal and becomes *engaged* to that man.

   (b) If a woman is engaged and later gets a proposal from someone who is higher on her list than the person to whom she is engaged, she becomes unengaged to that person (ditches him) and becomes engaged to the man she loves more. The man she has ditched does not get engaged in this round.

   (c) If a woman is engaged and later gets a proposal from someone who is lower on her list than the person to whom she is engaged, she turns down that proposal and the man who made the proposal does not get engaged in this round.

   (d) If a woman gets no proposals, she just waits for later rounds.

2. In round 2, each man who is not engaged proposes to the woman who is second on his list.

   (a) The women act as in the first round.

3. The algorithm continues with additional rounds (each unengaged man proposes to his third choice, and so on) until everyone is engaged. The number of rounds is limited since each man can make only n proposals (one to each women), and by then he will have proposed to any woman who has not already become engaged. Once a woman becomes engaged, she is always engaged to someone.

We do not prove here that the final matchings are stable. But with a little bit of reasoning you can see that the above unstable situation with Sarah, Sam, Janet, and John could not occur because if John prefers

---

Sidebar

An interesting research problem is: can we find an algorithm that will produce stable marriages, but which is fairer to both the women and the men? A related question is: what do we mean by fair? For example, what would be a "fair" set of marriages for Adam, Bob, Carrie, and Doris?

If these questions got you thinking about what such a fairer algorithm might be, just realize that someone can think about designing algorithms without thinking at all about bits, bytes, kilohertz, or *if* statements.

Sarah to Janet, he would have proposed to Sarah before he proposed to Janet, and so he would have ended up with Sarah and not Janet.

You may have noticed that this algorithm is **sexist**. There might be more than one set of stable marriages possible, and in that case, this algorithm produces marriages that favor the men's preferences. For example, suppose we have just two men, Adam and Bob, and two women, Carrie and Doris. Suppose the rankings are

Adam	(1) Carrie	(2) Doris
Bob	(1) Doris	(2) Carrie
Carrie	(1) Bob	(2) Adam
Doris	(1) Adam	(2) Bob

Now if we carry out the algorithm, in the first round Adam would pick Carrie and Bob would pick Doris. Everyone would be matched and the algorithm would complete. Both men got their first choice, but both women got their second choice.

If we had let the women do the proposing, both women would have gotten their first choice and both men would have gotten their second choice.

You might think that no one would care if this particular algorithm is sexist. However, when the algorithm is used to assign medical residents to hospitals, the hospitals play the role of the men in the algorithm and the residents play the role of the women. The algorithm gives the hospitals' choices preference over the residents' choices. An article in the 1981 New England Journal of Medicine complained about this inequality ("An Analysis of the Resident Match", NEJM 304:19 (1981) pp 1163-1166). Nevertheless, in 2004 the Association of American Medical Hospitals, which oversees the assignments, claimed that more than 83% of the residents obtained one their top three choices of hospital.

Computer scientists often have a bit of fun by defining algorithms in a seemingly silly way, as with the stable marriage problem, even when the algorithm has practical applications.

Sidebar

It has been shown that the difficulty of breaking the internet encryption system is directly related to another difficult problem we are all more familiar with: *factoring large numbers.* In school you probably tried your hand at factoring small numbers. For example the factors of 35 are 5 and 7 because

$$35 = 5 * 7$$

You might have memorized the factors of many small numbers, but you were probably not told in school that it is very difficult to factor large numbers. For example, suppose someone gave you the number 3337. How would you determine that its factors are 47 and 71?

Although mathematicians have studied the factoring problem for many years, there is no known way to factor a number that is significantly faster than trying all possible factors until we find the first one that evenly divides it. And since the problem of breaking the internet encryption system is closely related to the factoring problem, and since mathematicians have concluded that the factoring problem is (most probably) very hard, it is generally agreed that breaking the internet encryption system is (most probably) also hard.

4.2 Complexity

We have seen two examples of problems that have *easy* algorithms: searching, and stable marriage. In Chapter 2, we also saw an example of an algorithm that takes a very long time – the algorithm for breaking the internet encryption system. As we said, it is not known if there is an algorithm for that problem that has a smaller complexity, so we do not know for sure the complexity of the problem of breaking the internet encryption system. But many smart people have tried to find a faster algorithm without success, so it is generally believed that there is no faster algorithm. If you could prove that there is no faster algorithm, or if you could find a faster algorithm, you would become famous.

We are happy that this algorithm is hard because we do not want a computer to be able to do it. But there are other problems that we would really like to solve for which all known algorithms are impossibly hard. One such problem is the problem of scheduling production lines in a factory. But we are going to talk about another such problem, which is a bit more fun: playing chess. (By the way, if you are not a chess player, the same reasoning applies to most board games.)

Before we discuss the chess playing problem, we should point out that there are problems for which it has been proved that all algorithms for those problems are impossibly hard. We do not discuss any of these problems.

4.2.1 Playing Chess

There is an algorithm for playing chess that is easy to describe, but takes an impossibly long time. Just try all possible moves.

> First try (in your head) all possible moves you can make from the present position, then all possible replies your opponent can make, then all possible responses you can make, and so on, until all the possible games that can be played from the present position come to an end, as a win, a loss, or a stalemate. Then pick the move that wins for you, no matter what responses the opponent might make.

It is not known whether or not this algorithm will always lead to a win for White or Black from the starting position.

Of course, the number of possible moves, counter-moves, etc. is astronomically large, so the problem is computationally *infeasible* (impractical). You might be asking: if there is no practical algorithm for playing chess, how do people play chess? And how do computers play chess?

Let's talk first about people. Since there is no practical algorithm for playing chess, any strategy that a player uses is not an algorithm and is not guaranteed to win even if such a win is possible. One such strategy is

> From the current position, the player thinks about all possible moves she could make, then all replies the opponent could make, etc. But she cannot look ahead all the way to the end of the game. So after she has looked ahead some number of moves, she evaluates the position the board would be in then:
>
> - How many pieces would she and her opponent have?
> - What would be the locations of those pieces?
> - How many squares would those pieces control?
> - How important are those squares?
>
> Based on the answers to these questions, she picks a move.

In other words, the player uses her knowledge of chess strategy, her experience, and her intelligence.

How then do computers play chess? The field of computer science that attempts to make computers do things that people can do, but for which there are no practical algorithms, is called **Artificial Intelligence**. Building computer chess programs has always been an important challenge to the field of artificial intelligence. Computer chess programs use a strategy similar to the one used by some people. Because of their processing power and speed, they can look ahead more moves, but they do not have the same skills as a human in evaluating the positions reached after some number of moves.

Figure 4.2: *Deep Blue*

In 1997 an IBM program called Deep Blue beat the reigning world chess champion, Gary Kasparov, in a six game match. Kasparov had previously been undefeated, never having lost a chess match. The whole country became excited about the contest, which was reported in all the daily newspapers as well as on the internet. The team that created Deep Blue was awarded the $100,000 Fredkin Prize, which had been established in 1980 by Edward Fredkin from Carnegie Mellon University for the first computer program to beat a reigning world chess champion.

We talk more about Artificial Intelligence in Chapter 8.

4.3   Computability and Non-Computability

We have seen some problems that are easy for computers to do and some problems that are hard for computers to do. Are there any problems that are impossible for a computer to do? The question is:

> *Are there any fundamental limits on what computers can do, limits that apply to any computer – past, present, or future – no matter what components it is built from, how big it is, how powerful it is, how fast it goes, how much memory it has, or how long we are willing to wait for it to finish?*

The answer to that question is yes! We said in Section 2.2.1 that there are certain problems that are non-computable. Now we can make that statement more exact.

Sidebar

In the movie "The Hitchhiker's Guide to the Galaxy", super-smart beings create a computer to answer the ultimate question of life, the universe and everything. Solving this problem takes that computer a very long time. The answer, after all that time, is 42. The beings then create a computer (Earth) to find the question.

From this story, we can see that computers can take a really long time to produce unsatisfactory solutions to problems. Sometimes, the problem itself is ill-defined. Other times, the algorithm to solve the problem, or the program for that algorithm, are incorrect. We call this "garbage in, garbage out". Other times, we are just unsatisfied with the solution for aesthetic or emotional reasons.

Computers are used to find answers to "ultimate" questions in physics, chemistry, biology and mathematics. Do you think a computer could ever be smart enough to answer the "ultimate" questions of life?

There are certain problems for which there are no algorithms.
Those problems are said to be non-computable.

We have to be a bit more precise by what we mean by a **problem**. A problem is said to be **well defined** if it has a specific set of inputs and a specific set of correct outputs that are determined by those inputs. For example, the problem of searching a contact list is well defined. The inputs are a specific contact list and a name to be searched for, and the correct output is whether or not the name is in the contact list (and the phone number). By contrast, the problem of determining whether some particular person will always pay his credit card bill on time is not well-defined. The inputs are that person's credit history, financial information, etc., but there is no correct answer based on these inputs. Maybe, at some time in the future, he will get sick. Maybe he will lose his job. Maybe he won't.

There is obviously no algorithm for solving a problem that is not well defined. And we do not say that such problems are non-computable. (However, some computer scientists do work on problems that are not well defined. For example people who work in financial computing apply *data mining* and statistics to predict such things as whether or not some particular person will pay his credit card bill on time.)

But as we shall see, there are certain well-defined problems for which there are no algorithms. Those are the problems that are said to be non-computable.

When we say that a problem is non-computable we do not mean that the problem is really hard and we haven't yet figured out an algorithm for it, but maybe we will be able to think up an algorithm in the future. We mean that we can make a mathematical proof that no such algorithm exists. We are not going to give any such proofs in this book.

You might think that non-computability is just some abstract mathematical concept and all the non-computable problems are complex problems that only mathematicians can understand. But that is not true. There are many simple problems that we would really like a computer to be able to solve that are in fact non-computable. We give a short list of such non-computable problems that are related to designing and testing programs. There is no algorithm that can:

- Tell whether or not two given programs are equivalent (that is, they produce the same output for all inputs).

- Tell whether or not a given program will ever stop when given a specific input. (We have all seen our computer freeze up and do nothing. That is because some program inside the computer will never stop.)

- Design a set of test cases that will tell whether or not a given program will do what it is supposed to do (that is, whether or not it has a *bug*).

If these problems were computable and programs existed that could perform these tasks, software would be much more reliable than it is today.

You can see from these examples that many of the tasks that computer scientists do (or try to do) every day are non-computable. That is good news! If there is no algorithm for doing your job, you will probably not be replaced by a computer in the near future.

4.4 Shafi Goldwasser: Algorithms for Cryptography

When we discussed problems for which all known algorithms take an impossibly long time, we used breaking the internet encryption system as an example. **Cryptography** is the study of encryption systems. Shafi Goldwasser is a world leader in that field. She has also made important contributions to other areas of algorithms and theoretical computer science.

Her Life Shafrira Goldwasser was born in New York City in 1958. She received a B.S. in Mathematics at Carnegie Mellon University in 1979. She did her graduate work at the University of California at Berkeley and received her M.S. degree in 1981 and her Ph.D. degree in 1983, both in computer science.

Then she took a faculty position at M.I.T., where she in now the RSA Professor of Electrical Engineering. The RSA professorship was named after Ron Rivest, Adi Shamir, and Leonard Adelman, who invented the RSA system that is used for internet encryption. The RSA professorship

Name: Shafi Goldwasser
Born: 1958
Accomplishment: World leader in complexity and cryptography

was established in 1997, and Shafi was the first person named to that position.

Shafi is also professor of mathematical sciences at the Weizmann Institute in Israel.

Shafi is married and has two children.

What She Accomplished Although Shafi has made contributions to a number of areas in complexity theory and cryptography, she is perhaps best known as the co-inventor of *zero knowledge proofs*, by which someone can prove that they have some piece of information without revealing that information. For example, I can prove to you that I know the shortest route from my house to your house, without revealing what that route is. Although this kind of proof might sound very strange, it is actually quite useful in many advanced cryptography systems used on the internet.

Shafi has twice won the Godel prize in theoretical Computer Science, first in 1993 (the first time the prize was given) and then again in 2001. In 1996 she won the Grace Murray Hopper Award for "outstanding computer professional of the year." In 1998 she won the RSA Award in Mathematics for "outstanding mathematical contributions to cryptography."

In 2004 Shafi was elected to the National Academy of Sciences, and in 2005 she was elected to the National Academy of Engineering, both very prestigious positions.

Stories About Her One interesting comment that Shari has made about her interests in life is

> As a child, I loved literature and wanted to be a famous writer. Later, it became clear that my gifts lay more with numbers than with letters. Who knows? Maybe someday I'll go back and try to realize my childhood dream.

Chapter 5

Computer Security

Computers are becoming an increasingly important part of our lives. We buy things using computers; we communicate with each other using computers; we do our banking using computers; some people vote in elections using computers. While we are doing all this, computers around the world are gathering a large amount of information about us. Quite a bit of this information is (or should be) private. For example, most of us do not want even our friends to be able to Google our bank account balances, our credit card numbers, or the prescription drugs we have taken.

We might not think much about it, but we are very dependent on these computer systems being *secure*. For example, we don't want a bad guy to be able to:

- Break into a computer that has information about us and either steal some private information or change the information that is there.

- Eavesdrop on our communication over the internet and perhaps steal our credit card number.

- Perform some action on a computer system by pretending to be us, such as withdrawing money from a bank.

- Impersonate some computer system, such as an internet site, so that when we interact with that system, we inadvertently give that bad person some private information.

- Place a virus or other malicious software on our computer.

The part of computer science that deals with bad guys doing bad things with computers is called **computer security**. Computer security is important because computers know a lot about us, and because computers are networked (talk to each other a lot). In this chapter we

Sidebar

Maybe you want to make your computer secure against your brother. Suppose you keep your diary on your computer, and you don't want your brother to be able to read it. Just download some encryption software and keep the file containing your diary encrypted. Then it will be your secret forever.

Google the words "encryption freeware" to find Web sites that will allow you to download free software for encrypting files. Download and install the software, and then you can encrypt the file containing your diary.

talk about how computer security is used when you buy things over the internet and in computer voting.

5.1 Buying Things Over the Internet

Suppose you go to the American Girl Web site and want to buy something with a credit card. Some of the security issues are:

- **Authentication**: How do you know it is really the American Girl Web site you are interacting with and not some college students in a dorm room pretending to be American Girl in order to steal your credit card number? And how does American Girl know you are you and not a thief using your credit card number? You need security at both ends of the transaction.

- **Key Distribution**: How can you ensure that no one can steal your information while you send it to the American Girl Web site? You can encrypt it, but American Girl will have to be able to decrypt it. How do you find out what encryption key to use to send American Girl an encrypted message and what decryption key to use to decrypt messages sent by American Girl?

We will talk a little about these issues, and point you to some places where you can learn more. But there are also many other possible security issues involved in such a transaction. For example, maybe you have a virus or spyware on your computer that records every key you press, and sends it to someone else. Or maybe someone can break into the American Girl database and steal your information.

First let's take a quick look at encryption systems. There are two types of encryption system: symmetric encryption systems and asymmetric encryption systems.

1. In **symmetric encryption systems** the same key is used for both encryption and decryption. Symmetric encryption systems require much less computer power than asymmetric encryption systems, so

they are used whenever large amounts of data have to be encrypted. In particular they are used to encrypt your credit card information.

2. In **asymmetric encryption systems** different keys are used for encryption and decryption. Asymmetric encryption systems are used for a number of specialized applications such as authentication and key distribution, which are important when you shop.

Now we discuss how each of these encryption systems are used when you buy something.

Each time you want to send credit card information to a store, your browser and the store's Web site agree on the symmetric key that will be used for the encryption and decryption during that particular session. That key is called a **session key**. After one session, the session key is discarded. A new one is chosen each time. This is like changing the combination on your combination lock in school every time you go to school.

How do your browser and the store's Web site agree on the session key to be used for each session? This is the key distribution problem. This is where asymmetric encryption systems come in.

A Web site like that of American Girl owns a pair of asymmetric keys. The **private key** is kept secret by the site. The **public key** is made public for all to use. The simplest use of asymmetric encryption systems is that the public key is the encryption key. Anyone can ask the site for its public key, and then send that site an encrypted message using that key. Only that site can decrypt the message because only it has the private key.

You might think that there is no key distribution problem involved in this communication, but there is. For example, some bad guys might hijack a Web site, redirecting your browser to their own site behind the scenes. How do you know that when you ask the American Girl site for its public key, you are really talking to the American Girl site and not some students in a dorm room, who will gladly send you their public key?

So now you see how the authentication and key distribution problems are related. You must authenticate that the site you are talking to is really what you think it is before you can use the public key it sends you.

One more issue, even if you are talking to American Girl and the site sends you its public key, someone might intercept the message containing the public key and substitute its own public key. So we need one more idea to make the whole thing work.

Suppose that some site, say Sarah, which owns a pair of asymmetric keys, uses its private key as the encryption key and its public key as the decryption key. Now Sarah can encrypt a message with its private key, and anyone with the public key can decrypt it. Of course, that message

Figure 5.1: *A digital certificate? Of course, it doesn't really look like this.*

is not at all secret, since anyone can decrypt and read it. But any person who reads that message knows that only Sarah could have sent it, since it was encrypted with Sarah's private key.

We say that Sarah has signed that message with a **digital signature**. Such digital signatures play the same role that ordinary written signatures play in the paper world. Everyone will agree that Sarah actually sent that exact message, and Sarah cannot later deny having sent the message. (We have actually left out some of the details of digital signatures, but you can get the idea.)

One important application of digital signatures is **certificates**. There are some companies called **certification authorities**, who are in the business of certifying that a particular public key belongs to a particular Web site. Suppose American Girl wants to obtain a certificate for its public key. It sends that public key to the certification authority, which takes whatever action is required to determine that the site that sent that key is really American Girl, perhaps using a telephone or paper mail. Then the certification authority produces an electronic certificate containing the name "American Girl" and American Girl's public key, and it signs that certificate using the certification authority's private key. It then returns that certificate to the American Girl site.

In everyone's browser is the public key of the certification authority, so if a store sends your browser its certificate, your browser can use that public key to decrypt the signature, verify that the certificate is correct, and determine the store's public key. Note that all users have to trust the certification authority to correctly authenticate the sites to which it gives certificates. (Users also have to trust their browser to have the correct public keys for the certification authorities.)

Now we can put all this together and see how you actually buy something safely online. The complete protocol used is called the SSL (Secure Sockets Layer) protocol (again somewhat simplified).

Sidebar

To get some information about the certificate for the American Girl Web site, go the the checkout page of the store for that site `https://store.americangirl.com/checkout.php?p_key_code=` The address in the location bar at the top of the page starts with https, instead of http. This means it is a secure page. If you are using Internet Explorer, you should also see a locked padlock on the bottom right part of the page. You can double click on the padlock to obtain information about the certificate for the American Girl Web site. If you are using a different browser, you have to use a different method to obtain the information about the certificate. Look in the help file for that browser.

---

1. Your browser asks the American Girl site for its certificate.

2. When the browser receives the certificate, is uses the public key for the certification authority (which it has stored) to authenticate that the public key it received actually belongs to American Girl.

3. The browser selects at random a session key to use for this session with American Girl, and sends that session key to the American Girl site encrypted with American Girl's public key.

4. After the American Girl site receives and decrypts that message, a session key has been established.

5. The browser can then send your credit card number encrypted with the session key.

This protocol does a good job of authenticating the Web site and selecting a secure session key. To be precise, it does not authenticate that the site you are talking to is actually American Girl; it does authenticate that the public key received by the browser is actually American Girl's public key. If the site you are talking to is not American Girl, it will not be able to decrypt the messages sent to it.

The protocol does not do a very good job of authenticating the user. The protocol does not request a password or other authentication from the user. This means that anyone who knows your credit card number can impersonate you and buy things. Of course, when you use the telephone to order something with a credit card, the exact same statements about weak authentication can be made.

Many Web sites do require stricter user authentication. For example, your Web-based email program also uses the SSL protocol to establish a session key. Then it requires you to supply a password, which is sent after the session key has been established. Since the password is sent in encrypted form, it cannot be stolen by a bad guy. Thus the email Web site has been authenticated by its certificate and you have been authenticated by your password.

Research is still being done to design other protocols that have stricter authentication for both users and merchant sites.

5.2   Dorothy Denning: Wrote the Book on Computer Security

Dorothy Denning literally wrote the book on computer security. Her book, *Cryptography and Data Security* (published in 1982), was the first textbook in the field and is still a classic.

Her Life   Dorothy Elizabeth Robling was born in Grand Rapids, Michigan in 1945. In 1967, Dorothy received her bachelors degree in mathematics from the University of Michigan. She was training to be a high school mathematics teacher, but a summer job after her junior year aroused her interest in computers. She continued at the University of Michigan and got her masters degree in mathematics in 1969. She married a fellow student, Bill Davis, and they moved to Rochester, New York, where Dorothy worked as a systems programmer at the University of Rochester.

After her marriage broke up in 1972, she went to Purdue University where she earned a Ph.D. in computer science in 1975. During her first semester at Purdue, she took a course in operating systems, which ignited her interest in computer security. The course was taught by a young professor, Peter Denning, who married Dorothy in 1974. Dorothy has two two step children, Anne and Diana, from Peter's first marriage.

What She Accomplished   Dorothy was a faculty member at Purdue from 1975 to 1983. In 1980 she established a new graduate course in computer security, and in 1982 she wrote her classic textbook, "Cryptography and Data Security," for use in that course.

Dorothy worked at SRI International in Menlo Park, CA from 1983 to 1987 and at Digital Equipment Corporation's Systems Research Center in Parlor Alto from 1987 to 1991. In 1991, she took a job as professor and chair of the Computer Science Department at Georgetown University in Washington, D.C. In 2000 she was named Director of the Georgetown Institute for Information Assurance, and in 2001 she was named Patricia and Patrick Callahan Family Professor of Computer Science. In 2002, she moved back to California and became a professor in the Department of Defense Analysis at the Naval Postgraduate School.

During her career, Dorothy has written four books and more than 140 articles in professional journals, newspapers, magazines, and conference proceedings. She has testified before Congress on encryption policy and cyber-terrorism. She was the first President of the International Association for Cryptologic Research.

Name: Dorothy Denning
Born: 1945
Accomplishment: Wrote the Book on Computer Security

Among the awards she has received are the the 2001 Augusta Ada Lovelace Award, the 2001 *Time Magazine* Innovator Award, the 2003 Information Systems Security Association Hall of Fame Award, and the 2004 Harold F. Tipton Award for her outstanding information security career.

Stories About Her Donn Parker, another computer security expert, says of Dorothy,

> I don't know anybody in information security who is better in both writing and lecturing about extremely complex concepts so simply and so straightforward.

Dorothy has been an active advocate of ensuring that legal authorities can gain access to even encrypted (coded) information. For example, she has said,

> I believe that government access to communications and stored records is valuable when done under tightly controlled conditions which protect legitimate privacy interests.

5.3 Security in Computer Voting

The paper ballot system used in Florida in the 2000 presidential election caused a national uproar and increased the pressure for states to use computer voting systems. Because of the crucial importance of elections in our society, the use of computer voting brings up some important computer security issues.

When people use the term "computer voting", they are thinking of two kinds of systems:

Figure 5.2: *Why can't e-voting be as easy and secure as using an ATM?*

1. Internet voting, where people can vote at home on their PCs or perhaps in libraries and schools, and have their votes sent over the internet to some central computer, where they are counted.

2. Voting on computerized voting machines in polling places.

The security issues for internet voting are very complex and involve authentication and encryption, among other things. We will discuss only voting on machines in polling places, where those issues are less important. But even in that case, there are more security issues than we can discuss. We will discuss only the issue of how system insecurities can allow a bad person to change the votes in the computer. Some such insecurities are:

- The software (or hardware) was built by a dishonest person in such a way that that person or one of his friends can change the votes to favor a particular candidate.

- The software (or hardware) was built by an honest person, but the design or implementation has certain flaws, which result in "holes" in the system so that a dishonest person can somehow change the votes to favor a particular candidate.

- The hardware and software were built by honest people and there are no holes in the system, but the voting machine containing the software is left unguarded for some period of time before or after the election and a dishonest person can sneak in and replaces part of the software or hardware so that votes can be changed to favor a particular candidate.

You might think that the first two of these issues would not be so serious if the software were adequately tested. That's partly true. For example, in many projects that develop life-critical software for medical or space applications, over one half of the entire time of the project is devoted to testing. And the result is usually highly reliable. But remember:

- Designing a set of tests that completely tests a software systems and determines that it does exactly what it is supposed to do is an example of a non-computable problem, for which there is no algorithm. Therefore it is very difficult to develop a good set of tests or to know whether any specific set of tests is sufficient.

- If one of the security concerns is that the manufacturer of the voting system or some of its employees might be dishonest, why would you trust them to test the software? You might think that you could require that the testing be done by an independent group. However, that group would have to examine the software, and many manufacturers of voting machines view their software as proprietary and do not allow anyone else to examine it.

Most computer scientists believe that the best way to ensure that software is secure is to make it public, or "open source", and hence available for the entire software community to examine, test, and try to break. But most manufacturers of computer voting systems have refused to do this. In Australia, the first generation of computer voting software (eVACS) was open source, inexpensive and reliable. It was used in a national election. However, later versions are not open source.

Another issue has to do with paper ballots and manual recounts. If the only counting of the votes is done by the software in the computer, it would be impossible to perform a recount of the votes if people suspected that some bad thing had taken place. One suggested approach involves paper copies of the ballots. After the voter completes her vote, the machine would print out a paper copy of the ballot. That paper would be shown to the voter behind a glass shield so the voter can verify its correctness. Then the machine would put the paper into a container within the machine so that all the paper ballots could be manually counted if necessary (perhaps some randomly selected fraction of the machines would always be recounted). Only a small fraction of the current generation of voting machines produce paper copies of the ballots.

Even though many states have bought computer voting machines and used them in elections, it is generally agreed within the computer science community that there ought to be strict technical standards for such

machines and that the current generation of voting machines would not
meet those standards. A considerable amount of research over many
years will be required to first develop those standards and then to build
machines that can meet those standards. And secure internet voting
requires even more research and creative ideas.

In an interesting and easy to read paper, "Three Voting Protocols:
ThreeBallot, VAV, and Twin", the computer scientists Ronald Rivest and
Warren Smith discuss three voting methods that could making voting
more secure. You can download this paper from the internet for free.
None of these voting methods requires the use of a computer, but each
method is an algorithm. Computer scientists can use the analytical techniques they rely on to do more than just computer science – to have an
impact in areas as diverse as politics, economics, the health care system
and education.

5.4 Barbara Simons: For Honest Voting

Barbara Simons' career in computer science got off to a very slow but
fascinating start. She didn't get her Ph.D. until she was forty years old.
But she became a world-renowned expert on electronic voting and one of
the most influential computer scientists in the country.

Her Life   Barbara Ann Bluestein was born in Boston, Massachusetts
in 1941. Barbara started an undergraduate degree in Mathematics at
Wellesley in 1958. There she (re)met her future husband Jim Simons,
who was studying for his Ph.D. at M.I.T. (His parents had lived in the
same apartment building in Brookline, Massachusetts in which her parents lived, and he claims to have attended her second birthday party.)
She became engaged to Jim in the spring of 1959 and, when Jim went
to the University of California at Berkeley to continue work on his Ph.D.,
she transferred to Berkeley.

At the beginning of her sophomore year at Berkeley, Barbara and Jim
eloped to Reno, Nevada. A year later they had their first child (Barbara
was only nineteen!). In 1961, at the end of her junior year, Jim received
his Ph.D. and went off to teach at M.I.T. Barbara followed him to Brookline without getting her degree. She says she never even thought of
staying behind at Berkeley to finish her degree. "Women didn't do that
sort of thing in those days." During the next nine years, she had two
more children and lived the life of a housewife and mother.

In 1968, when her husband accepted a faculty position at the State
University of New York at Stony Brook (yes, that's where we are both
from), Barbara moved to Stony Brook with him. When her marriage
broke up, her father suggested that she learn to program as a way to
support herself, since she had been good in mathematics. So she returned to school at Stony Brook in 1970. She took some undergraduate

Name: Barbara Simons
Born: 1941
Accomplishment: Publicized Issues of Computerized Voting

courses in computer science and then was accepted into the computer science Masters Program.

Before Barbara had quite finished all the requirements for the Masters degree, she moved to California when her then current boyfriend got a job there. She was accepted into the Ph.D. program at the University of California at Berkeley even though she had no university degrees whatsoever. Before she got her Ph.D. degree from Berkeley, she had to get a Masters degree (she says this is a commentary on how irrational bureaucracies can be). When she received her Ph.D. in 1981, she was forty years old.

What She Accomplished In 1980 Barbara joined the Research Staff at IBM's San Jose Research Center (now called Almaden). In 1992, she joined IBM's Applications Development Technology Institute as a Senior Programmer and subsequently served as Senior Technology Advisor of IBM Global Services. She has retired from IBM and is currently a Consulting Professor in Science, Technology, and Society at Stanford.

Barbara has done research in a number of areas, including scheduling theory, compiler optimization, and fault tolerant computing and has authored or coauthored two books and many technical papers. But she is probably best known for the active role she has taken with respect to electronic voting.

She was a member of the National Workshop on Internet Voting that was convened by President Clinton and produced a report on internet voting in 2001. She also served on the Security Peer Review Group of the Department of Defense Secure Electronic Registration and Voting project. She has testified before both the U.S. and the California legislatures and at government-sponsored hearings. She served on the National Science Foundation panel on Internet Voting and the President's Export Council's Subcommittee on Encryption. She is co-writing a book on voting machines.

Barbara was president of the Association for Computing Machinery (ACM), the main professional organization for computer scientists in the USA, from 1998 to 2000. She was the third women to serve as President of the ACM since it was founded in 1947. The other two were Jean Sammet (1974-1976) and Adele Goldberg (1984-1986). After Barbara's term, Maria Klawe served as president from 2002 to 2004. In 1993 Barbara founded the U.S. Public Policy Committee of the ACM, for which she was chair or co-chair for many years.

Barbara has received many honors. She is the first woman to receive the Distinguished Engineering Alumni Award from the College of Engineering at U.C. Berkeley (in 2005). She is a fellow of the ACM and of the American Association for the Advancement of Science. She has been featured in Science magazine, CNET, and Open Computing.

Several of the awards Barbara has received have been for her work on ethics in computer science. In 1992 she was awarded the Norbert Wiener Award for Professional and Social Responsibility in Computing. She has also received awards from the Computing Research Association, the ACM Special Interest Group on Computing and Society, and the Electronic Frontier Foundation.

Stories About Her   Barbara Simons, in a talk at Butler College in 2002, had the following advice:

1. Never take no for an answer, if what you want to hear is yes. Find someone else in the chain of command who might say yes.

2. Take things one step at a time. I never would have gone back to school to get a Ph.D. in computer science. It would have been far too intimidating. But I could go back to school to learn to program. And I could stay in school in order to achieve the very next goal – pass a course, pass some exam, etc.

3. People make regulations, and people can bypass them. (See item 1).

Chapter 6

Databases

6.1 What is a Database?

You have probably heard the word *database* before, but you might not realize that you own at least one database – your address book. A database is just a collection of data. You use your address book database to do the same kinds of things that all computer databases do:

- You add new items to it.

- You query it to find a specific email address or phone number.

- You gather information from it, for example counting how many friends you have.

Of course most computer databases are much larger than your address book and have stricter performance requirements. For example, two of the largest computer databases belong to Google and Visa.

- The database for the Google search engine contains information about more than 1 trillion web page addresses (URLs). In June 2008 it processed more than 7 billion searches, and this number increases almost every month.

- The database for the Visa credit card company contains information about more than 1.2 billion credit card holders. Every day it processes more than 100 million credit card transactions worth more than $5 billion. In addition, there are very strict requirements for the accuracy and correctness of the data stored within it.

6.2 What Do People Do With Databases?

Databases are used in at least three different ways. We explain these three ways using the Starbucks coffee chain as an example.

Figure 6.1: *What information does the database on your MP3 player contain? What are the 'transactions'? How do your MP3 player and online music store use this information to suggest what you might buy?*

Transaction Processing: Databases frequently store information that describes the current state of an enterprise. For example, each Starbucks maintains a database of the prices and current inventory of all the items it sells as well as the amount of money in all its cash registers. That information corresponds to the state of the enterprise. When an event happens in the real world that changes the state of the enterprise, a change must be made to the information stored in the database. These changes are made in real time by programs called **transactions**, which run when the real-world event occurs.

Say you buy some coffee and a special mug at Starbucks. This transaction is started by the clerk at the checkout counter using the cash register, which interacts with the database.

> One cafe latte and an insulated mug were purchased; compute the price, print out a receipt, update the balance in the cash drawer, and subtract these items from the store's inventory.

You would be surprised if the transaction did not complete in a few seconds.

The main goal of a transaction processing system is to make sure the database continues to represent an accurate model of the real world as events occur in the real world. In this case, the event is your purchase, and the real-world situation is the store's inventory and the amount of cash in the cash drawer.

Other transaction processing systems you have interacted with are the ATM machines in a bank, the Visa credit card system, and the Web sites at which you have bought things.

Decision support: The main goal of decision support is to run mathematical analyses of the data stored in one or more databases, to help humans make decisions. For example, the Starbucks management might want to analyze the data stored in the databases in Starbucks cafes to help them decide which stores to keep open and which to close. Such decision support applications are becoming increasingly important as enterprises attempt to turn the *data* in their databases into *information* they can use to advance their long-term strategic goals.

Often, decision support queries are quite complex and cannot be efficiently executed against the local databases. Starbucks probably has a separate database just for complex decision support queries. The database might contain historical information about sales and inventory from all Starbucks branches for the past several years. This information may be extracted from the individual cafe databases at various times and updated once a day. Such a database is called a **data warehouse**.

A manager can enter a complex query about the data in the data warehouse, for example:

> During the winter months of the last five years, what is the percentage of customers in the northeast who bought insulated mugs at the same time as they bought a drink?

Perhaps in cold regions, insulated mugs should be placed near the checkout in the winter.

Data Mining: A manager might also be interested in making a much less structured query about the data in the data warehouse, for example:

> Are there *any* interesting combinations of items bought by customers?

Such queries are called **data mining**. In contrast with decision support, in which requests are made to obtain specific information, data mining can be viewed as knowledge discovery – an attempt to extract new knowledge from the data stored in the database.

Data mining queries can be extremely difficult to formulate and might require sophisticated mathematics or techniques from the field of artificial intelligence. A query might require many hours to execute and might involve several interactions with the manager for obtaining additional information or reformulating parts of the query.

One widely repeated story about data mining (that might be an urban myth) is that a convenience store chain used the above query ("Are there *any* interesting combinations ...") and found an unexpected correlation. In the early evenings, a high percentage of male customers who bought diapers also bought beer – presumably these customers were fathers who were going to stay home that night with their babies.

Decision support and data mining are becoming increasingly important as companies look for ways to benefit from the large amount of data they have about their customers. As one simple example, when you log onto your gmail account and then surf the internet, Google keeps track of the pages you have visited. This information and the content of the emails you send and receive is used to select the ads that you see on many web pages (not just Google web pages). Many people are concerned about some of the possible less benign uses of such information.

Sidebar

Data Mining in the Real World

- After 9-11, the United States government started using data mining techniques to eavesdrop on phone conversations between people in the the United States and people in foreign countries. We do not know for sure what data mining techniques were used, but we can guess that these were among them: (1) *networking* where records were kept of the people who were contacted, the people those people contacted, and so on, to find the network of people communicating with each other, and (2) *keywords* where certain keywords, such as terrorist, bomb, etc. were searched for. There was a considerable discussion in Congress and in the media about the legality of doing that eavesdropping without first getting a warrant.

- Many schools, libraries, and parents use internet porn filters, based on data mining technology, to prevent children and teenagers from looking at pornography on the internet. Often these filters use keywords to identify porn sites. In one famous example, one of the keywords used was *breast*, and students were unable to get information about breast cancer because all the relevant pages were blocked.

Do you think schools and/or parents should use porn filters or other methods to restrict the pages you can see on the internet?

6.3   Relational Databases and SQL

As you can probably see by now, the basic ideas behind databases are very simple. However, making it all work can be a bit more complicated.

The data in a database is stored in **tables.** For example, this table describes (some of) the students in a school.

Students	Id	Name	Address	Status
	111111	Kathy Smith	123 Main St.	Freshman
	222222	Mary Jones	234 Broadway	Junior
	567890	Jodi Susser	567 Southway	Senior
	445678	Barbara Simpson	444 Rowe Rd.	Freshman
	323359	Sarah Martin	335 Peak St.	Sophomore
	111122	Kathy Owens	444 Whamer Lane	Junior

The name of the table is **Students**. Each row of the table contains information about one particular student. Each column in the table describes that student in some particular way. At our university, a **Students** table would require more than 15,000 rows.

Tables are accessed and updated using the Structured Query Language (SQL). One example of an SQL statement is

```
SELECT Name
FROM Students
WHERE Id = '567890'
```

which queries the Students table to return the Name of the student whose Id is 567890. It returns Jodi Susser. Other examples of SQL statements are

```
UPDATE Students
SET Status = 'Senior'
WHERE Id = '22222'
```

which changes the Status of Mary Jones from Junior to Senior,

```
INSERT INTO Students
VALUES ('654321', Flo Doe, '111 N St', 'Senior')
```

which inserts a new row in the table for Flo Doe, and

```
DELETE FROM Students
WHERE Id = '323359'
```

which deletes the entry for Sarah Martin.

There are other kinds of SQL statements and more complex forms of the SELECT, UPDATE, INSERT, and DELETE statements. For example

```
SELECT Id, Name
FROM Students
WHERE Status = 'Freshman'
```

returns a whole table containing the Ids and Names of all Freshmen:

	Id	Name
	111111	Kathy Smith
	445678	Barbara Simpson

The complete database for a school would contain many other tables in addition to the Students table. For example, there might be a Courses table containing information about each course taught in the school, and a Transcript table containing the grades each student got in the courses she took. A shortened version of the Transcript table might look like this

Transcript	Id	Course	Semester	Grade
	111111	Math1	F-2005	B
	445678	Math1	F-2005	A
	567890	Math1	F-2005	A
	111111	English1	S-2004.	A
	445678	English1	S-2004.	B
	567890	English1	S-2004	A

Note that the Id in this table is the Id of a student and is the same Id as in the Students table. The Transcript table does not include the student's name or other information about the student, since that information is already in the Students table and it would be inefficient to include the same information in two tables.

Some queries might require information that is stored in more than one table. For example, we might want to print out some transcript information about all the Freshman, and some of that information might be in the Students table and some in the Transcripts table. The `Select` statement

```
SELECT Name, Course, Grade
FROM Students, Transcript
WHERE Status = 'Freshman'
```

selects information from the Students and Transcript tables and produces the table:

	Name	Course	Grade
	Kathy Smith	Math1	B
	Kathy Smith	English1	B
	Barbara Simpson	Math1	A
	Barbara Simpson	English1	B

which includes the requested information about the two freshman.

The Relational Model This model of a database as a set of tables is called the **relational** model because it can be described and analyzed using the concept of a **mathematical relation**, which has been widely studied in the mathematics community. Each table can be described as a relation. The `Select` statements we have been discussing can be viewed as performing mathematical **operations** on those relations.

There is a mathematical theory that describes how these operations can be combined, interchanged, and so forth. This theory can be used by the designers of queries to make those queries more efficient and by the implementors of the database management system to make the queries execute more efficiently.

The mathematical theory underlying databases is one of the most elegant and useful parts of the database field. Algebraic operations and mathematical theorems become database design tools. You really appreciate mathematics when you see how it applied in the real world.

6.4   Indices

A nice feature of SQL databases is that when you want to search the database for some information, you can just write a `SELECT` statement describing the information you want. You do not have to give the computer detailed instructions about how to search the tables to find that information. The database management system itself decides how to perform the search. We say that SQL is **declarative**, not **procedural**.

Let's spend a little time discussing how the system might perform such a search. For example, suppose we want to search for all the Freshman in your school using the `SELECT` statement

```
SELECT Id, Name
FROM Students
WHERE Status = 'Freshman'
```

How can the system perform that search? One approach would be to search the entire Students table, one row at a time, keeping track of all the rows for which the status entry is Freshman. That certainly would work, and some kinds of searches require such a search. But remember, in our school there are 15,000 students. And in some applications, the tables are even larger. The customer table for some businesses might have hundreds of thousands of rows. Searching such a table, one row at a time, would take a very long time.

Another approach would be to define an **index** on the Students table. An index contains the locations of all the rows in the table that satisfy the index entry. We might use the CREATE INDEX statement

```
CREATE INDEX StudentsStatus on Students (Status)
```

to create an index called StudentsStatus on the Status column in the Students table. That index keeps track of the location of all the rows for the different statuses: Freshman, Sophomore, Junior, and Senior. After an index has been defined, the system automatically creates and maintains it. Then when a SELECT statement is executed that can use that index, the system automatically uses the index to perform the search.

We can define more than one index for the same table. For example, we might define two indices on the Transcript table, one on Course and one on Semester.

```
CREATE INDEX TranscriptCourse on Transcripts (Course)
CREATE INDEX TranscriptSemester on Transcripts (Semester)
```

A particular query might involve more than one index. For example, the query

```
SELECT Name
FROM Students, Transcript
WHERE Status = 'Freshman' AND Course = 'Math1'
```

which returns the Names of all the Freshman who took Math1, involves the index on Status in the Students table and the index on Course in the Transcript table.

The data structures that store the indices can become very large and complex. The theory and practice of how indices should be constructed, how they should be updated as the database changes, and how they should be used by the system in implementing the searches specified by SELECT statements is an important part of database technology.

6.5 Jennifer Widom: Database Researcher

Jennifer Widom is a well known researcher and textbook author in the database field.

Name: Jennifer Widom
Born: 1960
Accomplishment: Database researcher and author

Her Life   Jennifer Widom was born in Ithaca, New York in 1960. In 1977 she set off to study trumpet at the Indiana University School of Music. In 1982, she received an interesting degree called "Bachelor of Science in Music with Outside Fields in Mathematics and Computer Science." In 1983 she received a Master's degree in computer science at Indiana, and in 1985 she received another Master's degree in computer science from Cornell. In 1987 she received a Ph.D. degree in computer science from Cornell.

From 1987 to 1993, Jennifer was a Research Staff Member at the IBM Almaden Research Laboratory in California. In 1993 she joined the faculty of Stanford, where she is now a Full Professor in the Computer Science and Electrical Engineering Departments.

Jennifer is married to Alex Aiken, who is also a computer science professor at Stanford. They have two children.

What She Accomplished   Jennifer has coauthored several books and published over 150 technical papers on various aspects of databases and other areas of computer science.

Stories About Her   Jennifer is an avid traveler, together with her husband and later joined by their children. In the late 1990s she wrote several informal articles about adventure travel with young children. In 2007-08 her family took a full year off from work and school to travel the world by sailboat, camper and hiking, as well as more traditional means.

Chapter 7

The Internet

You probably use the internet several times every day: to read your email, IM your friends, do your homework, play a game, go on YouTube, MySpace, or Facebook, or just do a Google search. You might think that the internet has been around for a long time. Not true. The internet became available for commercial use in 1991. (What year were you born in?) Before that, it had just been available for government and university use. To give you some idea of how fast the internet is growing:

- In 2008, there were more than 162 million Web sites. That number was 100 thousand in 1996.

- In July 2008 people watched more than 1 billion videos per day on YouTube. YouTube was founded in 2005.

- In June 2008, Google ran more about 233 million searches per day. Google was founded in 1998.

In its short lifetime, the internet has had a profound effect on how we all lead our everyday lives and on how our society works. And the internet is still expanding, becoming faster and running even more applications. So how does the internet work?

7.1 Communication: How Computers Talk To Each Other

A computer can talk to another computer by sending it bits over a communication network, for example a phone line. In order for the second computer to understand what the first computer is saying, they must agree on what the bits mean. We might say they must agree on the language that will be used for the communication. Technically, this language is called a **communication protocol**.

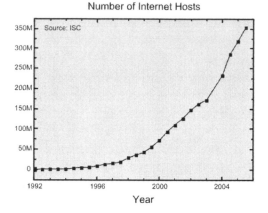

Figure 7.1: *Number of internet hosts in your lifetime*

The internet is based on a set of standard communication protocols. Any computer that has been programmed to understand those protocols can talk to any other computer that has also been programmed to understand those protocols. The computers might have been made by different vendors, for example, Dell or IBM, and they might use different operating systems, for example, Windows or Unix. As long as they understand the standard internet protocols, however, they can talk to each other over the internet. That's a real advantage of the internet.

The word internet refers to the fact that a large number of networks from all over the world are interconnected to make the internet. New networks and new users can be added at any time as long as they understand the standard internet communication protocols.

internet Addresses   One part of the standard protocols is the **internet address**. Every computer on the internet has both a **host name** and an internet address (actually an **IP** or **internet Protocol Address**). Phil's computer at work has the host name: *sbpml.cs.sunysb.edu.* The host names should be read backwards:

> *edu* means that the computer is at an educational institution.

> *sunysb* means that the institution is the State University of New York at Stony Brook.

> *cs* means it is at the Computer Science Department.

> *sbpml* is the name of the computer.

The suffix, *cs.sunysb.edu*, is sometimes called the **domain name**, and the entire host name, *sbpml.cs.sunysb.edu*, is sometimes called the **fully qualified domain name**.

You can compare a computer address to a postal address. Post office workers also read your address backwards: first the zip code, then the state, then the city, then the street address, and then your name.

When someone wants to send a message to a computer, they can refer to it by its host name. The internet contains computers called **name servers**, and that person's browser sends the host name to a name server, which replies with the IP address. For example, the IP address of sbpml.cs.sunysb.edu is *130.245.1.39*. The browser then uses the IP address to send the message. The internet contains computers, called **routers**, which act as post offices to ensure that each message goes to the proper address.

Addressing Individual Pages   So how do we refer to an individual page that we want to download from an internet site? Suppose you want to download the shopping cart page from the T J Maxx internet site. The host name for the T J Maxx site is *www.tjmaxx.com*, where

> *com* means that it is a commercial site
>
> *tjmaxx.com* is the domain name
>
> *www* is the name of the computer

If you were to send that host name to a name server, you would find that the IP address of that host at the T J Maxx site is *64.95.84.94*.

You might be surprised that *www* is the name of the computer. Since most sites have a host name that begins with *www*, you might have thought that *www* was part of some internet protocol. Not so. It is just customary for sites to name the computer that provides the webpages *www*. Because of this, there are many computers named *www*.

Not all sites name their computer *www*. The host name for the main page of the Microsoft Network is *www.msn.com*, but if you want to shop for gifts on the Microsoft Network you go to *shopping.msn.com*. Both sites have the same domain name, but they are hosted on different computers, one named *www* (with IP address 207.68.183.32) and the other named *shopping* (with IP address 65.54.157.252).

Individual pages on the internet are referred to by their **URLs (Uniform Resource Locator)**. The URL of the home page for T J Maxx is
```
http://www.tjmaxx.com/home.asp
```
Such URLs should be read backwards:

> *home.asp* is the name of the file on the host computer that contains the description of the initial page
>
> *www.tjmaxx.com* is the host name where the file exists
>
> *http* is the protocol used to send the page (HyperText Transfer Protocol) (https would mean that the page was sent in encrypted form).

Whenever a Web page is displayed in your browser, its URL is shown in the location bar at the top of the screen.

As a somewhat more complex example, in the URL for the shopping cart page at the T J Maxx site,
```
http://www.tjmaxx.com/checkout/basket.asp
```

Figure 7.2: *A router takes packets and forwards them*

the host name is the same as before, *checkout* is the name of a folder on the host computer, and *basket.asp* is the name of the file in that folder that contains the shopping cart page that is to be downloaded.

If you want to download the shopping cart page, you refer to it by its URL. The browser then sends the host name part of the URL to a name server to find the IP address of the T J Maxx site. Then it sends the T J Maxx site a message containing the URL, and the software at the T J Maxx site looks at the last part of the URL and knows to send you the shopping cart page. Your message to the T J Maxx site contains your return address, and the T J Maxx site replies to your messages using this address. After the T J Maxx site sends you the shopping cart page, it disconnects from your site.

Cookies   As you purchase items from T J Maxx, you send messages to the T J Maxx site containing information about those items. The T J Maxx site replies to each message by sending you an updated version of the shopping cart page. After sending you each updated version, the T J Maxx site disconnects from your site. That brings up the question,

> If the T J Maxx site disconnects from your site every time it sends you a message, how does it remember what you have previously put into your shopping cart so that it can send you the updated version of the shopping cart page?

The first part of the answer is that the T J Maxx site maintains a database, in which there is a record corresponding to your partially filled shopping cart. But that brings up the additional question,

> When you send the T J Maxx site a new message with another item you want to order or ask to checkout, how does it know which record in its database corresponds to your shopping cart?

The answer is a **cookie**. Each time the T J Maxx site sends you a message, it puts a cookie in your browser (invisibly to you). The cookie is a block of a few hundred bytes of information that identifies the record in T J Maxx's database corresponding to your shopping cart. The next time you send a message to the T J Maxx site, the site can access the cookie and get the information about your shopping cart record in its database.

A cookie is something like the ticket you get when you check your coat in a restaurant. The number on the ticket is meaningless to you, but when you return the ticket to the coat-check attendant, she can use the number on the ticket to find your coat.

Cookies have other, less benign uses that involve gathering information about you and your activities on the internet and have been the subject of much controversy. We discuss this issue later.

URLs for Web pages can be more complex than these examples. In addition to Web pages, other resources available on the internet also have URLs. In the T J Maxx example, such resources might include, for example, a picture to be downloaded with a catalog page.

Packets That's the basic idea of the addressing portion of the internet communication protocols. But now you might ask the question,

Why is communicating over the internet so inexpensive?

After all, you pay one low price to your internet provider each month, and you can send messages on the internet all over the world. You don't have to pay anything extra even if you send a hundred digital photographs to your cousin in Latvia. By contrast, if you want to call your cousin on the telephone, you would have to pay many cents a minute, and it would cost you a lot more than when you call your sister who lives down the street. Why? The answer lies in the **protocol**.

When you call someone on the phone, a connection is established between your phone and hers. You essentially are renting that connection for the duration of the call. For example, while you are thinking and not talking, the connection is idle and no one else can use it. That is a waste of resources. By contrast, on the internet, when you are sending a message to your cousin in Latvia, you are sharing the communication lines to Latvia with many other people. The internet protocols break up your message, which might be a sequence of hundreds of thousands of bytes, into a sequence of **packets**, of a few hundred to a few thousand bytes each. Then those packets are sent separately to your cousin interleaved with the packets of other people who are also sending messages.

Each packet includes information about the address to which that packet is being sent, and internet routers make sure it gets to the right address. So eventually all the packets get to the right destination and can be put back together to reassemble the message. All of this is of course invisible to you – you are just sending a message. But while the packets are being sent, they are interleaved with the packets for other messages going to other addresses. Therefore, while you are thinking or not sending packets for some other reason, the line is available for other users. In fact, your message to your Latvian cousin uses only a tiny fraction of the capacity of the communication lines on which it travels. That's why it's so inexpensive to send messages over the internet.

Sidebar

A Brief History of the Internet
The idea of packet switching was invented in 1961 by Paul Baran of the
RAND Corporation. It was reinvented in 1965 at the National Physical
Laboratory in England by Donald Davies, who first used the words "packet
switching." Much of the theory underlying packet switching was developed
by Leonard Kleinrock at MIT in 1964 and later at UCLA. His laboratory at
UCLA was the first node of the Arpanet.

Arpanet went online in 1969. The basic communication protocols that
made the internet possible were developed in 1973 by Robert Kahn, at
Bolt Beranek and Newman in Boston, and Vinton Cerf, at Stanford University. The first commercial use of the internet was allowed in 1991, and
commercial companies started to operate the internet in 1995.

That same idea can be used to send telephone voice messages over
the internet. The voice message is first converted into a sequence of
bytes. This sequence of bytes is then broken into packets, which are
sent using the usual internet protocols. When the packets are received,
the bytes in each packet are converted back into a voice message.

When this approach was first used, it had one shortcoming. As each
packet in the sequence is received, it is converted back into voice. But
if a packet is delayed because of heavy traffic on the internet, when it is
converted back into voice, its sound is delayed and the voice might sound
distorted and unnatural. However, as the capacity and speed of the
internet has increased, and as more and more people have broadband
connections to the internet, this shortcoming has virtually disappeared.
Many companies are now offering commercial phone service using this
technology at a very low price. The number of land lines in the USA grew
most years until 2000. Since 2000, the number of land lines has dropped
each year, due to the increasing use of cell phones and broadband.

Packet-based communication has another big advantage. Since packets are automatically routed from computer to computer around the internet, if one computer happens to be down, the packets can just be
rerouted on a different path using different computers. So it is highly
likely that your message will get to its final destination, even if some
of the computers on the network are down for some reason. This type
of reliability was an important goal of the Arpanet, the predecessor of
the internet. The goal was to make the network reliable for military
communication even though parts of the network had been destroyed or
disabled by some terrorist or enemy organization. The outcome is that
the internet is highly reliable for commercial use and for just plain fun.

7.2 Hypertext: Jumping From Place to Place

Before we tell you what hypertext is, think about how you get more information about some topic when you are reading a book. First, you might look up the topic in the index to see if it is discussed in other parts of the book. If you want even more information, you might look up the topic in a dictionary or encyclopedia. All of this is boring and hard work. Now think of what happens on the internet. You can just click on a word on one page and immediately go to any of hundreds of other sites that give you more information about that word. That's what hypertext is.

The original concept of hypertext was invented 25 years before it was used on the internet. The word **hypertext** was coined by Ted Nelson at Vassar in 1965. It refers to text in which individual words in one document are linked to other documents that give additional information about those words.

In 1990 this concept was used by computer scientist Tim Berners-Lee, then a software engineer in Switzerland, to invent many of the internet ideas we now take for granted:

- Web pages that can be downloaded from a site to a local user and can contain words that are linked to other Web pages (hypertext).

- A language, called HTML (HyperText Markup Language), which can be used to prepare Web pages containing hyperlinks (usually called just links) to other Web pages. We give an example of HTML below.

- The Web browser that displays Web pages written in HTML and automatically performs the linking to other pages when the appropriate words are clicked.

The part of the internet that includes these three ideas is called the **World Wide Web**. Interestingly, one person, Tim Berners-Lee, can be said to have invented the World Wide Web in 1990.

Other parts of the internet, for example email and instant messages use different communication protocols.

An example of a statement with a hypertext link that might be displayed by your browser is

To see your T J Maxx shopping cart, please click <u>here</u>

The link is the underlined word *here*. When you click on the word *here*, the browser goes to the T J Maxx home page at the above internet address, and a program at that site downloads the shopping cart page. One question you might ask is: how does the browser know where to go to find the page. The answer lies in the HTML language. The HTML statement that was downloaded to your browser that caused it to display that statement is

To see your T J Maxx shopping cart, please click
<a href = http://www.tjmaxx.com/checkout/basket.asp> here
</a>

The URL of that page at the T J Maxx Web site is included in that HTML statement and is associated with the word *here* by the HTML statement

<a href = URL of the page> word to be underlined </a>

But that HTML statement is not shown on the screen when the browser displays the statement. Only the underlined word *here* is displayed.

The HTML language has other features besides linking to pages at other sites. For example

- It describes the format of the information displayed on the screen (what type font will be used, is the information to be displayed in the form of a list or some other structure, etc.).

- It allows you to input information, for example in a text box on the shopping cart page, that will be sent to the site when you click on some button.

- It allows pictures and other information to be displayed on the page from other files at the site that sent the page.

- It includes programs that will be run in your browser while you are looking at the page, for example an animation program that causes a cartoon animal to dance around on the page.

If you want to make your own Web page, you either have to learn the HTML language or use some software tool that will automatically generate HTML for you.

7.3   Buying Things On The Internet

One type of HTML statement that is used when you buy things over the Web causes a submit button (or a button with a similar name) to be displayed on your screen. When you click on that button, the browser sends a message back to the Web site that sent you the page. That message includes all the information that you filled in on the page. The message causes a particular program to run at that site to process the information you sent. Now let's see how to buy something over the Web.

1. You give your browser the URL of the merchant, and the browser sends a message to that address requesting a reply.

2. That message causes a particular program to run at the merchant's site. That program prepares an HTML page and sends it back to your address.

3. Your browser displays that page.

4. You fill in some information on the page and then click on the submit button, which causes your browser to send the information back to the merchant's site.

5. That information causes another program to run at the merchant's site.

6. That program processes the information you sent and prepares a new HTML page, which it sends back to your address.

7. Messages are sent back and forth until your purchase transaction is complete.

8. The merchant's site uses cookies to keep track of your partial order and other information about you.

As we said in Section 2.2.1, some of these messages are encrypted so that an intruder can't eavesdrop on the communication and steal your credit card number. Also, unknown to you, during the interaction the merchant's site might communicate with other sites, for example a credit card company's site to approve your purchase.

7.4 Email and Instant Messaging

That's a quick summary of how that part of the internet works. Other parts of the internet, for example email and instant messaging, work a bit differently and use different protocols. Of course all these protocol differences are hidden from the user by the browser.

Although email uses a different protocol, the addresses are similar. Your address specifies a **mail server**, which is like a post office to which emails addressed to you are sent and held until you ask to read them. For example Phil's email address is *pml@cs.sunysb.edu* where

pml is his name

@ means the rest of the address is the host name of his mail server

cs.sunysb.edu is the host name of the mail server

Again, the host name of the mail server is sent to a name server that provides the appropriate IP address.

Email is said to be a **client-server** application, because your mail is sent to a **mail server**, after which your browser acts as a **client** to that server and retrieves your mail.

By contrast, instant messaging is said to be a **peer-to-peer** application. When you want to IM someone, an IM server gives your browser the IP address of that person and gives that person's browser your IP address. After that, the two browsers use these IP addresses to send

---

Sidebar

Email was first available on the Arpanet (the predecessor to the internet) in 1971. Email users used the SNDMSG program developed by Ray Tomlinson at Bolt Beranek and Newman (and yes, addresses had the @ symbol).

The first successful instant messaging system, ICQ (I seek you), was introduced by the Marablis company in 1996.

---

messages directly back and forth to each other without any further communication with the IM server. We say that the two browsers are peers and are communicating peer-to-peer.

Many of the file sharing systems such as Kazaa and Grokster, which are used to share music or movies (either legally or illegally), also operate in a peer-to-peer fashion.

7.5   Searching the Internet with Google

In addition to buying things, sending email, and instant messaging, people also use the internet to search for information. There are actually two kinds of internet sites that provide facilities for searches. Some sites just gather a large amount of information in a conventional database and then either provide that information for free or charge for it. For example, our university maintains a subscription to the Web of Science database. This means that faculty and students are allowed to query the database to get information about technical publications. For instance, you can ask it to provide a list of all the publications about internet protocols published in the years 1998 through 2000.

But the technically most interesting search facilities are those provided by search engines such as Google. You can enter a list of search words and almost instantly get a list of internet sites related to those words. We will discuss Google in some detail.

Don't think that when you enter your list of search words, the Google search engine begins searching the internet for matches. Google has previously built a huge database that it searches to provide the matches for your request. So how is that database built? Google maintains over 450,000 computers. At any instant in time some large number of these computers are acting as robots, called **spiders** or **GoogleBots**, which crawl around the internet gathering Web pages to be put into the database. When one of these GoogleBots finds a page, it follows the links on that page to find still more pages. It is estimated that Google indexes pages from more than 1 trillion web addresses.

The Google database consists of two parts. The first part stores all the pages it has gathered. The second part is an index to those pages. The index is like the index in the back of a book. It contains a list of words, and for each word, it contains a list of all the pages on which that word appear. Google indexes every word in every page in its database.

For example, if you search using the keyword *genie*, Google will return a list of all the pages in its database that contain the word genie. When we looked, that list contained a total of 16,200,000 pages. If you search using the keywords *magic genie*, Google will return a list of all the pages that contain both the words magic and genie, 2,650,000 when we looked. And if you search using the keywords *"magic genie"* Google will return a list of all the pages that contain the word magic followed by the word genie, 61,900 when we looked. To convince you that Google indexes every single word, even "the" and "a," we searched on *"the magic genie"* and got an entirely different number of pages (890) and on *"a magic genie* and got a still different number of pages (11,100).

You might ask how Google determines in what order to return the pages in its list of pages. Google seems to be quite good at making the page you want be one of the first few pages on the list it returns. That's one of the things that distinguishes Google from the other search engines. What good is a list of 16,200,000 pages returned for my keyword *genie*, if the page you want is not one of the first few on the list?

Google uses a number of methods, some of which are proprietary, to determine which pages are probably the most important answers to your particular query. Are the keywords in the address of the page? Are they in the title of the page? Do they appear at the beginning of the page? Do they appear many times in the page?

And, the most interesting method, the method that distinguishes Google from the other search engines is called **PageRank**. PageRank is a set of methods for evaluating the relative importance of pages based on the number of other pages that link to them. The PageRank method was developed by the two Stanford Ph.D. students, Larry Page and Sergey Brin, who later founded Google in 1998.

The idea of evaluating the importance of Web pages based on the number of pages that link to them is related to the way our Computer Science Department rates the research papers written by faculty members. We evaluate the contents of each paper, but we also judge the importance of the paper by counting the number of papers written by other authors that reference that paper – the number of *citations* for that paper. Similarly the PageRank algorithm says that a Web page is probably important if that page has many other pages with links to that page. We might say that those other pages are voting for that Web page.

For each Web page stored in the Google database, the PageRank algorithm keeps track of how many other pages have links that point to that page (how many other pages are voting for that page). A key idea in the algorithm is that if one of these other pages has many outward links, the algorithm assumes each link is less important than if it has fewer links. If we say that those outward links are the votes of that page, then if a page makes many votes, each vote does not count as much as if it makes fewer votes. Using ideas such as these, the PageRank algorithm ranks

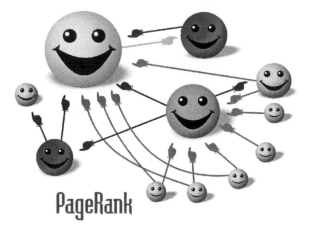

Figure 7.3: *PageRank, as visualized by Felipe Micaroni Lalli*

all the pages that satisfy your request, and that information is used to determine the order in which those pages are displayed.

You might also ask how Google returns its results so fast. Think of the amount of computation it must perform. It must look up your keywords in its index, determine which pages returned from the index satisfy all your keywords, rank those pages based on their relative importance in satisfying your query, prepare the page to be sent to you, and then send it. And you are not the only one Google is dealing with. As we said, Google can handle 3000 requests per second. How can it do it all so fast? Part of the answer is its 15,000 computers. But the real answer is that it utilizes very sophisticated algorithms developed by very sophisticated computer scientists. Google employs some of the best computer scientists in the world.

7.6   Marissa Mayer: Google Goddess

Marissa Mayer is the Vice President for Search Products and User Experience at Google. She is largely responsible for Google's simple yet elegant Web user interface and has overseen the development of such Google products as Google News, Froogle, and Google Desktop Search.

Her Life   Marissa Ann Mayer was born on May 30 1975 in Wassau, Wisconsin. In high school she was the star of the debating team, the captain of the cheerleading squad, and the valedictorian. Her debating team won the Wisconsin state championship, and her cheerleading squad was the state runner up. She spent eight years studying ballet.

She went to college at Stanford, where she intended to study to become a physician. But the courses bored her, and she looked around for another major. She discovered computer science and a professor who

Name: Marissa Mayer
Born: 1975
Accomplishment: Google Goddess

made her love the subject. In 1997, she received a B.S. with honors from Stanford in symbolic systems, a program that emphasizes computer-human interaction and artificial intelligence. In 1999 she received an M.S. in computer science, also from Stanford.

When she was ready to graduate, Marissa began to look for a job. She talked to two Stanford graduate students, Larry Page and Sergey Brin, who were thinking of starting a new company to be called Google. "I know about those Stanford Ph.D. students," she says. "They love to Rollerblade. They eat pizza for breakfast. They don't shower much. And they don't say 'sorry' when they bump into you in the hallway."

What She Accomplished In June 1999, Marissa joined Google as a programmer. Google had just been founded in 1998, and Marissa was approximately the 20th employee.

While at Google, Marissa became the technical leader of the user interface team and is now responsible for all of Google's Web products. She has responsibility for almost everything the Google user sees, from the look of the Web pages to the software underneath the pages.

Marissa's views on the Google user interface can be summarized in this quote taken from an interview she had with Mark Hurst in 2002

> Google should be "what you want when you want it," as opposed to "everything you could ever want, even when you don't."
>
> I think Google should be like a Swiss Army knife: clean, simple, the tool you want to take everywhere. When you need a certain tool, you can pull one of these lovely doodads out of it and get what you want. ... Like when you see a knife with all 681 functions opened up, you're terrified. That's how the other sites are – you're scared to use them. Google has the same level of

complexity, but we have a a simple and functional interface on it, like the Swiss Army knife closed.

The utmost thing in the user experience [is] to have the most useful experience. It's important to differentiate between "usefulness" and "usability." At Google we make a "useful" tool and then we put a "usable" interface on top of that. One has to precede the other. If you have usability without a useful product, you don't really have much.

Part of Marissa's job is to help decide which of the new initiatives bubbling around in the company should get the attention of the two founders, Larry Page and Sergey Brin. An important factor in Google's success is their policy of giving their employees up to 20% of their time to develop their own ideas. One of Marissa's responsibilities is to meet with the employees working on these ideas and decide when, if ever, these ideas are worth pursuing at the product level.

Stories About Her   In her job, Marissa must interact with both the technical people and the sales and marketing people (the Ph.D.s and the M.B.A.s). She feels comfortable with both groups. A former employee says, "She's a geek, but her clothes match."

Marissa needs to travel a lot for her job, but the rumor is that she flies only on red-eyes (planes that fly coast-to-coast overnight) so she never has to miss a business day.

In addition to her full-time job at Google, Marissa has taught introductory computer science courses at Stanford to over 3000 students. She has received both the Centennial Teaching Award and the Forsythe Award for outstanding contributions to undergraduate education.

Part of Marissa's ambition comes from her grandfather, who was crippled by polio at the age of seven, but built up an insurance company and served for thirty years as mayor of Jackson, Wisconsin. "I saw my grandfather triumph in the face of adversity," Marissa says, "and I don't have any such obstacles to overcome."

Marissa is single and has a hobby of flying kites. She can often be seen flying one of her three parafoils over Marina Green in San Francisco.

7.7   The Computer Catches a Virus

What's good about the internet is that you are connected to the whole world, and your computer can access files and information from computers anywhere. What's can be bad about the internet is that the whole world is connected to your computer, and computers from anywhere can access files and information from your computer. Intruders can break into your computer and make it do things you do not want it to do. We briefly discuss some methods that intruders can use to do this.

Sidebar

The first use of the term (computer) *virus* was in the 1972 science fiction movie *Westworld*, 20 years before viruses appeared for real.

The first use of the term *worm* was in the 1975 science fiction story *The Shockwave Rider* written by John Brunner.

Viruses A virus is a program that attaches itself to another program, and whenever that other program runs, the virus runs too. For example, a virus might be attached to a spreadsheet program and run whenever the spreadsheet program runs. When the virus runs, it can do anything it is programmed to do. It almost always reproduces, copying itself and attaching these copies to other programs. When those other programs run, the copies of the virus also run and make even more copies.

Email Viruses An email virus is a particular type of virus that moves around from computer to computer as an attachment to an email message. When you read the email and click on the attachment, the virus runs. In addition to doing nasty things to your computer, it may collect email addresses from your address book and forward itself to those people. It might even use these email addresses as return addresses on the email it sends, to mislead the new recipients.

You might ask, how does clicking on an attachment cause the virus program to run? As you might know, files in Windows have extensions: for example .doc for Word files and .xls for Excel. When you click on a file, Windows looks at the extension of the file to determine what to do with the file: for example, open it in Word if it is a .doc file or in Excel if it is an .xls file. You might also know that the .exe extension corresponds to a program, and if a file has that extension, Windows assumes that file is a program and attempts to run it. So if the attachment to an email message is a file that has as .exe extension, Windows will run it. However, you might not know that there are a number of other extensions that Windows also assumes are programs and runs them: for example, .vbs, which corresponds to Visual Basic programs, .pif, .bat, .com, and .lnk, which are left over from DOS, the predecessor of Windows, and .scr, which is used for screensaver programs. Some viruses use these extensions in an attempt to fool the receiver of the email into thinking that clicking on such an extension will not cause a program to run. It is also true that Microsoft Office documents, such as Word and Excel, can contain programs within them (called macros), and therefore email attachments with .doc, and .xls extensions are also potential containers for email viruses. Incredible as it might seem, the default in Windows is that the file extensions are not displayed on the screen, so that it is not immediately obvious which mail attachments are programs.

Sidebar

The term *Trojan horse* comes from an ancient Greek legend. The Greeks captured the city of Troy (and also Helen of Troy) by hiding soldiers inside a harmless looking (but hollow) wooden horse. They left the horse outside the gates of Troy and the rest of the troops got into their ship and apparently sailed away. The saying, derived from that legend,

   Beware of Greeks bearing gifts

can be restated as

   Beware of Geeks bearing free software

Worms   A virus can run only if the user runs the program to which the virus is attached. However, a worm is a program that can run independently, without the user taking any action. Worms often depend on security flaws in the computer system, which allow unauthorized programs to enter the system and then run on the system.

When a worm runs on a computer, it does whatever it wants to do on that computer and also searches on the internet to find another computer that has the particular security flaw it knows about. Then it uses that flaw to copy itself onto that other computer and run there. It continues to replicate itself from that computer.

A worm can also send copies of itself as attachments to email messages. But when it is run from the attachment, the worm places copies of itself in places that allow it to run independently, for example whenever the computer is rebooted. It can then also send and receive files over the network using protocols other than email.

Because worms can run and reproduce on their own, they can infect many computers in a short period of time. For example, on July 19, 2001 the Code Red Worm infected more than 359,000 internet host computers in less than 14 hours. And during its peak period in mid-August 2003, the Sobig.F worm, which used email to send copies of itself to other computers, constituted 73% of all the email on the internet.

Trojan Horses   A Trojan horse is a program that is supposed to do one thing, but in addition does some other (unexpected) thing. For example a "free" software program that you downloaded might contain a Trojan horse program that disables your anti-virus software, so that at a later time, a virus program can enter your computer.

In the strict definition of a Trojan horse, a Trojan horse program does not replicate itself. However, many people would say, for example, that an email virus embedded as a macro in a Word document email attachment was a Trojan horse, even though that virus does reproduce itself.

Adware and Spyware   When you download "free software," you are usually required to click on a license agreement, and you probably don't even

---

Sidebar

A computer hacker is a person who breaks into computers, usually by writing a virus, worm, trojan horse, or malware. Some computer scientists are good computer hackers. They find weaknesses in computer systems. Then they work to fix those problems before a bad guy can exploit them.

For example, in 2005 Mark Russinovich discovered that Sony was putting programs on some of its music CDs that ran invisibly on your computer, told Sony what you were listening to, and made your computer vulnerable to bad hackers. Sony eventually repaid the customers who bought those music CDs and agreed not to use that software anymore.

Good computer hackers can even find bugs in software that has been used for a very long time. In 2008 Dan Kaminsky uncovered a way to get name servers to "lie" about the IP addresses for domain names. This is partly because name servers, like encryption protocols, rely on probabilities. However, name servers weren't using big enough probabilities.

So how does a good computer hacker help people? After finding this problem with the name server software, Dan Kaminsky thought of a way to fix the problem. He did not publish the problem he had found until the fix was implemented and was being used by as many companies as possible. This was a good thing – in July 2008 someone leaked an idea about the problem, and within days bad hackers were exploiting it.

Good computer hackers are often motivated by the admiration of other computer scientists. Both Mark Russinovich and Dan Kaminsky were able in the end to present their discoveries and get praise from their peers.

There are many computer scientists who find it exciting to guess how computer systems can be broken, and then fix those problems. Do you think it would be fun to be a good computer hacker?

---

read it. In some of these agreements, for example those for file-sharing software, you often agree to accept adware software as a part of the download. Adware runs along with the program you wanted. It downloads from the internet various kinds of advertising that displays, often as banner ads, along with the program you are running. That's perfectly acceptable. After all, the person who created that software has to make a living too, and if you agree to accept the adware, you should not object to seeing the ads. (Adware stands for advertising supported software.)

There is a bad possibility, though. Sometimes, along with the adware, one or more spyware programs are also downloaded. The fact that the spyware programs will be downloaded might have been in the license agreement or it might not. Some people would not call a program spyware if you agreed to its downloading.

Spyware programs can run at times other than when you are executing the original program you downloaded. When they run they transmit information about your activities back to some internet site (they phone home!). Although most spyware programs send only relatively benign information, they can monitor all kinds of activity, for example what sites you have visited, what you have bought on the internet, what email you have sent, and what chatroom conversations you have had. They can even log all the keystrokes you have made on your keyboard or change the contents of an email message after you have clicked the send button. In fact, since they are just like ordinary programs, they can do anything any other program can do. In particular they can try to disable your other programs that are attempting to detect them. A spyware program is like a worm in that it can run independently, but unlike a worm, it usually does not attempt to reproduce itself.

Cookies   As we discussed earlier, while you are interacting with some site, for example to purchase something, that site can place a cookie in your browser. The cookie contains information about you that the site can use to access its database to remember, for example, what you have in your shopping cart and what products you have looked at. You might think that after you have finished with that interaction, the cookie would be removed from your browser. But cookies are not necessarily removed when the interaction is over and can be accessed by that site the next time you visit it. Sometimes that is harmless. For example, every time you go to Amazon.com, that site uses their cookie to remember who you are, and it immediately suggests some books you might want to order based on books you have recently ordered.

But cookies can also be used for less harmless purposes, involving remembering the history of what sites you have visited. In order to make it more difficult to gather such history, browsers enforce the policy that only the site that placed a cookie can later read or write it. But that policy does not always have the desired effect. You might not realize that when a page displays a picture advertisement, that picture was probably not put there by the site you are visiting. Instead, many sites sell advertising rights to a company such as DoubleClick. When the advertising company's site places its ad, it can read or write a cookie specific to itself. So it can keep track of your visits to all the sites that use its ads. You might not want that information to be generally available.

Spam Email   Some companies have acquired huge databases of email addresses and are using them to send spam email messages. Often these addresses are obtained from "free offers" on the internet that require you to supply your email address. Then databases of these addresses are offered for sale. Email addresses can also be obtained by scanning Web pages to find sequences of characters that look like email addresses (for example, they contain an @ symbol).

Some companies don't even bother to purchases databases of email addresses. They just pick random sequences of letters and numbers and place them in front of @aol.com or @yahoo.com. Enough of these randomly generated email addresses match real addresses to make it

---
Sidebar

The term *spam* comes from the product of the Hormel Foods company called SPAM (Shoulder Pork and HAm), first introduced in 1937. Hormel has long since abandoned any hope of restricting the use of the word to describe junk email even though it maintains its copyright on the word to describe its product.

Although we do not know for sure when the term spam was first used for junk email, it is probably based on a famous 1970 "spam sketch" in Monty Python's Flying Circus. In this sketch, a waitress in a cafe describes what ingredients are in certain foods and repeats the word spam over and over again, after which a chorus sings "Spam, spam, spam, spam, spam, spam, spam, spam, lovely spam! Wonderful spam!"

---

worthwhile. The fact that communication is essentially free over the internet and therefore it costs these companies next to nothing to send a spam message makes the situation even worse. Spam is profitable if it gets a return rate of only 0.0025% (by contrast, traditional direct mail advertising requires a return rate of 2%).

In 2008, over 95% of all emails were spam (compared with 8% in 2001). By comparison about 40% of all United States postal mail is business marketing.

Malware   Any software that is specifically intended to damage or disrupt a computer is sometimes called **malware** (malicious software). How can you protect yourself from malware?

- Regularly check for and install updates to your operating system.

- Carefully read agreements you sign when downloading free software to check for adware and spyware.

- Use a firewall program to protect against worms.

- Use an anti-virus program to protect against email viruses.

- Occasionally run a program like CCleaner that can identify and remove known spyware and adware programs.

7.8 What's Next

The internet has been in existence for less than two decades. What will it look like after two more decades? No one knows for sure, but advances in technology that will certainly cause revolutionary changes.

- The speed at which you can send and receive information over the internet will be 1000 or more times more than it is now. (That is true now in experimental versions of the internet.)

- A million or more times as much information will be available over the internet.

- Your personal computer will be 100 times faster and will be able to store 100 times as much information as it does now.

- You will be able to access the internet wirelessly from any place in the world using hand-held computers with huge amounts of computing power and storage.

- Many new kinds of devices will be able to access the internet. Right now your laptop/desktop, cell phone, TV and gaming devices can use the internet. In the future, your car, fridge, microwave and maybe even your drinks cans will also have internet access.

- Artificial intelligence technology will allow the creation of software agents that are many times more sophisticated than those in existence today.

What kinds of new internet applications will be possible with these new technologies? What new things will you be able to do when you can access the internet wirelessly from anywhere in the world using some handheld device?

- You will be able to send a message to your microwave and tell it to start cooking your dinner.

- You will be able to watch your baby sitter taking care of your infant while you are at a restaurant.

- You will be able to find out the exact location of your child (or your spouse, or yourself) at any instant of time.

- You will be able to ask a software agent in your office to prepare a proposal for a customer while you are having lunch with him.

- You will be able to download a movie or a book in 3 seconds for a charge of $.99.

- You will be able to order a new prom dress over the internet. First you will look at a pre-stored picture of you photoshopped into a number of dresses. After you choose one of them, your measurements will be emailed to a factory where the dress will be custom made on an automated assembly line (by robots) and shipped in 24 hours.

- Your refrigerator will be able to order milk for you from the supermarket when you are running low.

That's just some of the things that people will be able to do. And what new things will businesses be able to do? And how will it affect education? And politics? You can help make it all happen.

Name: Sandy Lerner
Born: 1955
Accomplishment: Co-founder of Cisco Systems

7.9 Sandy Lerner: Cofounder of Cisco Systems

When Sandy Lerner was 29 years old, she and her husband Len Bosack founded Cisco Systems, which is now the world leader in networking products for the internet with an annual revenue of over $22 billion.

Her Life Sandra Lerner was born in 1955. Her parents divorced when she was four years old, and she was sent to live with her aunt and uncle on a California ranch. Here she learned to be independent and to love animals. During the summers she was sent to live with a wealthy aunt in Beverley Hills, where she took ballet lessons. But she remained a rebel at heart. She brags about crashing a pickup truck at age 12. She protested the Vietnam war at age 13. She started her business career at age 9, buying a steer, selling it and investing in two more. By the time she was 16, she had acquired thirty head of registered breeding cattle. The revenue the herd generated helped put her through college.

She graduated from high school at 16 and worked for a bank for a year and a half to make more money to go to college. It was at the bank that she first encountered sex discrimination: "The president would make us kneel on the floor, so he could check the length of our skirts."

Sandy first studied politics. In 1975 she got a B.A. in political science from California State University at Chico, and in 1977 she got an M.A. in government from Claremont. There she saw her first computer, which she said was a "religious experience." She moved to Stanford University to study computational mathematics and became part of a group of "very hard-core computer nerds." At Stanford met Len Bosack, who she married in 1980. "Len's clothes were clean, he bathed, and he knew how to use silverware. That was enough. I was enchanted." In 1981 she got an M.S. in statistics and computer science from Stanford.

What She Accomplished In 1981 Sandy became Director of Computing Services at the Stanford School of Business. Len worked five hundred yards across the campus as the manager of the the Computer Science Department's computer labs. The computers in each department were linked in a local area network, but the two networks were not linked to each other. So for example, Sandy and Len could not exchange email.

Sandy and Len decided to build a *router* that would allow messages on one network to be routed to the other. The network they built using these routers eventually interconnected about 5000 computers all around the Stanford campus. When other universities and research centers asked to buy routers, Sandy and Len asked Stanford to start building and selling routers, but Stanford refused.

So in December 1984, Sandy and Len started their own company and named it "Cisco," the second half of San Francisco. They ran the operation out of their house, and each room in the house was used for building, testing, manufacturing, or shipping. They financed the venture by mortgaging their house, using their credit cards, and persuading their friends to work for deferred pay.

They looked for venture capitalists to finance their company and after being turned down by more than seventy, they finally found one in 1987. By then, they were selling about $250,000 worth of routers a month. The venture capitalists insisted on putting in their own top management. Sandy had a falling out with the new managers. Both she and Len left the company in 1990 and began to sell their Cisco stock as soon as the company went public (also in 1990) for a total of about $170 million.

Stories About Her In 1990, Sandy and Len amicably separated. Sandy now lives in a 1000-acre cattle ranch, Ayrshire Farm, in Virginia. Len lives in Redmond, Washington. They set up a charitable foundation with 70% of their money. They remain friends and manage the foundation jointly. Some of Sandy's favorite charities funded through the foundation promote the humane treatment of animals. Some of Len's favorite charities are in the area of "alternate technologies." The foundation also bought an English manor that was once owned by Jane Austen's brother. Sandy turned it into a library and research center on 18th and 19th-century woman writers, called Chawton House.

In 1996 Sandy cofounded (with Wende Zomnir and David Soward) a different company Urban Decay (http://www.urbandecay.com), which produces women's makeup in colors such as purple and green that reflect the urban environment (supposedly because Sandy couldn't find the right shade of purple nail polish to satisfy her taste). The company's line of alternate colors for lipstick and nail polish was introduced with a memorable advertisement: *Does Pink Make You Puke?*.

Chapter 8

Artificial Intelligence

8.1 What is Artificial Intelligence?

In Chapter 4 we said that an algorithm is a step by step procedure that is guaranteed to stop and produce the correct answer. A large part of computer science is concerned with tasks for which there are efficient algorithms. These are tasks that computers can easily do and people can also easily do but often not as fast as a computer. But what about problems for which there are no efficient algorithms? Perhaps

- All algorithms for that problem take an impossibly long time, for example playing chess.

- The problem is not well defined, for example the problem of determining whether a person will pay his credit card bill on time.

In fact, many problems that people have to solve in their daily lives have no efficient algorithms. Examples include planning your daily activities, diagnosing an illness, figuring out what a sentence means, or playing the Chinese game "Go." One way of defining Artificial Intelligence, or AI, is to say that

> AI is the study of problems for which there are no efficient algorithms.

However, this definition is not complete. There are many problems that computers can't solve, and neither can people. One example is the problem of breaking the internet encryption system. These problems are not part of AI. The problems that are part of AI are problems that are hard for computers, but that people can solve using some attributes of human intelligence. So what are some of these attributes of human intelligence?

- **Knowing and reasoning:** Humans know a large number of things about a wide variety of different subjects. Think about all the knowledge you have about: clothes, food, the English language,

---

Sidebar

The first use of the term Artificial Intelligence was in 1955 in a **A Proposal for the Dartmouth Summer Research Project on Artificial Intelligence**, prepared by John McCarthy from Dartmouth, Marvin Minsky from IBM, Nat Rochester from IBM, and Claude Shannon from Bell Labs. Quoting from that proposal:

> *This study is to proceed on the basis of the conjecture that every aspect of learning or any other feature of intelligence can in principle be so precisely described that a machine can be made to simulate it.*

---

the neighborhood around your house, what it's like to be a girl, schoolwork, colors, animals, money, arithmetic, etiquette, how to act in a restaurant, and on and on. People are capable of acquiring new knowledge, of adapting easily to changing knowledge, and of using this knowledge to make sense of our world. Can we make a computer do these same things?

- **Perceiving and acting:** Humans have five senses through which they perceive the world. These perceptions, together with our knowledge and reasoning, often guide our actions. For example, we might see a person coming out of a store carrying a steaming cup and, since we know that cups often hold hot drinks, we might then go into the store in search of a cup of hot chocolate. Can we give a computer the powers of perception that we have, connect those perceptions to reasoning abilities, and use the result to give a computer the power to act in the world?

- **Learning:** The human brain is extraordinarily adaptable. We enter the world unable to walk, speak, read, buy things, add up numbers, or find our way around. But we learn to do all those things, and we can continue learning as long as we are alive. How can we give the computer the ability to learn based on its knowledge, reasoning ability, perceptions, and actions?

So AI deals not with any hard problem, but specifically with hard problems that reflect some aspect of human intelligence. We can say that

> *AI is the study of problems for which there is no efficient algorithm and whose "solutions" involve human-like intelligence.*

We put the word solutions in quotation marks, since there is no efficient algorithm for the problem. This means that even when we apply human-like intelligence, we cannot guarantee to obtain the "correct" answer.

8.2 Knowing and Reasoning: Computers Taking Chemistry Tests

At the core of many AI applications is knowledge or structured information about some subject, with some way of using that knowledge or reasoning about that knowledge. Computer programs that are based on knowledge and reasoning are called *expert systems*. These systems try to store the knowledge a person (an expert) has about some particular area and then imitate how that person would act based on that knowledge.

For example, suppose we wanted to make an expert system that a bank could use to decide whether to give a credit cared to a college student. We would ask the bank's credit officer what information she uses to make such decisions. She might say she uses

- The student's credit card history (from other credit cards).

- The student's work history of summer and part time jobs.

- The student's income from summer and part time jobs.

- The student's income from scholarships.

- The student's income from allowance (from her parents).

Then we would ask the credit officer how she uses that information to make her decision. We might ask her to summarize how she uses that information in a set of rules, for example,

- IF the student has had a job for at least a year AND the income from that job is greater than XX dollars AND the student's credit history is not bad, THEN approve the card

- IF the student's total income is less then YY dollars, THEN do not approve the card.

She might provide many rules, some much more complicated than these. We would then implement an expert system that used the information and the rules to imitate how the credit officer makes her decision. If we find that the system sometimes makes bad decisions, we would consult the credit officer, and update the information categories or the rules.

Knowledge and reasoning were the focus of most artificial intelligence systems throughout the 1960s and 1970s. Automatic computer reasoning systems have been used to solve some interesting problems. For example, in 1996 a computer was used in the proof of the Four Color Theorem, a theorem that had been worked on for over 100 years by humans without an adequate proof. Also, the expert system MYCIN, built during the 1970s, was better at diagnosing infectious blood diseases than most "regular" doctors and only a little bit worse than specialists.

Figure 8.1: *In ten years, will you teach the computer ... or will the computer teach you?*

However, knowledge and reasoning systems still aren't as "smart" as humans. They can't learn very well. They know about only one type of information. They aren't very good at explaining themselves.

In 2002 Vulcan, Inc., an organization founded by Paul Allen (who co-founded Microsoft with Bill Gates), started work on Project Halo. Project Halo's goal is to create a "digital Aristotle": a computer program that knows information about a lot of different things; can learn new information; and can explain itself. This program could be used to teach high school or college students or help scientific researchers.

The first Project Halo project was a 6-month competition. There were three teams: a team from Cycorp, a knowledge and reasoning company; a team from Stanford Research Institute and the University of Texas at Austin; and a team from Ontoprise, a small German company. Each team was given 71 pages of an AP chemistry syllabus. At the end of the six months (in 2003), each team gave Vulcan its computer program. Vulcan then gave each computer program an exam. The exam had three parts. First, there were 50 multiple choice questions. Then, there were two sets of 25 multi-part questions. Each computer program also gave explanations for its answers. Each program's answers were graded by human chemists. The answers were graded separately for correctness and for explanation quality. An example Project Halo competition question that you might know the answer to, is "Explain why the solution resulting from a strong acid and a weak base is acidic even though all of the base and acid have reacted".

The story of the competition's results is a little like "Goldilocks and the Three Bears". The Ontoprise team (the little bear) was the smallest and had the least experience. The Cycorp team (the papa bear) had decades of building knowledge and reasoning programs, and lots of existing computer programs and knowledge written down in databases. The SRI team (the mama bear) came somewhere in the middle.

The Ontoprise program finished the exam in 2 hours. The Cycorp program finished in 12 hours. The SRI program finished in 5 hours.

All three graders agreed that the SRI program got more answers correct than the Ontoprise program, which got more answers correct than

---

Sidebar

How would you like to have a computer tutor? Many people today work on computer tutors. Here are some examples:

- At the University of California at Los Angeles, computer scientists work with movie writers and actors to make a computer program that can teach soldiers how to be more culturally sensitive in peace-keeping situations.

- At the Tucker-Maxon Oral School, the Vocabulary Tutor with Baldi (a computer system with a talking head that can understand human speech) helps children who are deaf learn to read.

- At the University of Pittsburgh, a computer system that interacts using speech and can understand student emotions is used to tutor students in physics.

- The Educational Testing Service has a program called Criterion that teachers can use to grade student essays and give students writing feedback.

Computer tutors are always available, never bored, and always friendly. On the other hand, they may be a little slow, or not as creative as a human tutor. Would you like to use a computer tutor?

---

the Cycorp program. Two graders agreed that the SRI program gave better explanations than the Ontoprise program, and that the Ontoprise program gave better explanations than the Cycorp program.

After the first Project Halo competition, a much longer project was started and is still in progress. This project also involves three teams: the SRI team; the Ontoprise team; and a new team, Team ISX. In this project, the computer programs will learn AP chemistry, biology, and physics from textbooks and other resources.

8.3 Perceiving and Acting: Computers Driving Cars

One of the early dreams for AI was to create machines that could use their senses to get around in the world. Recently, this dream has come much closer to reality through projects such as DARPA's Grand Challenge project. There have now been three Challenge races, in 2004, 2005 and 2007. The history of these Challenges is just like the history of AI: big dreams, early failures, and eventual success.

The Challenges are races for "autonomous", or self-driving, cars. The people who run the Challenge secretly plan a race course and hold qualifying races for the cars that want to be in the race. The vehicles that qualify run the race and the first vehicle to finish wins a prize.

The first Grand Challenge race was in 2004. Fifteen vehicles were

Figure 8.2: *Stanford's Grand Challenge 2005 vehicle, Stanley*

selected from one hundred six entries to run the race. The prize was $1,000,000. The race course was 142 miles long over back roads (often dirt roads) in California and Nevada. Competing vehicles included:

- The Spirit of Kosrae, a Jeep Cherokee with multiple sensors and special software for route planning, from the company Axion, LLC.

- The Palos Verdes High School Road Warriors vehicle, an Acura MDX SUV with its interior removed and software and a generator added, from students at Palos Verdes High School.

- CajunBot, a 6-wheeled ATV with 3 computers and video, sonar and laser sensors added to enable it to self-navigate, from the University of Louisiana at Lafayette.

The race was a disaster; no vehicle made it further than 7 miles. Several vehicles didn't even get onto the course, but broke at the start line. One of the vehicles sensed small bushes near the road but interpreted them as big boulders, and backed away from them.

The second Grand Challenge race was in 2005. Twenty-three vehicles were chosen from one hundred ninety five entries. The race course covered 132 miles in the Mohave desert, and the prize was $2,000,000. This time, the race was much more successful. Five vehicles finished. The winning car, Stanley, came from Stanford University and finished the race in 6 hours, 53 minutes. The vehicles that placed second and third came from Carnegie Mellon University. The fourth and fifth vehicles to finish came from Louisiana and Wisconsin. The first four vehicles were "regular" cars, with special sensors and computer software; the fifth one was a construction truck, which is why it moved more slowly.

Let's look a little closer at the perception and action skills of Stanley, the prize-winning Grand Challenge 2005 vehicle. Stanley was a 2004 Volkswagen Touareg. It had 635 pounds of additional equipment, including several computers: a GPS (Global Position System) to help the

---
Sidebar

You can't easily use the ideas underlying expert systems to design a program that will drive a car, because even expert drivers can't explain how they drive a car.

There are many activities that people can do very well, but can't explain how they do them. If you play a sport or a musical instrument, think about how you would explain how you do them well. Could you do the entire explanation in writing, or would you need to use gestures and body postures in your explanation? These kinds of problems are among the most challenging for AI.

---

car plan its route; laser sensors to help the car perceive the road around it; gyroscopes and accelerometers to help the car keep its balance; radar for long distance seeing; and color cameras that act like human eyes. The laser sensors could sense the ground within 100 feet of the car. The video cameras could provide good pictures of distances up to 160 feet.

Stanley also had software for interpreting the input from the sensors and for learning based on the sensor input and on practice driving sessions. Stanley's programs included: a program, Mapper, for interpreting the input from the lasers; another program, Planner, for telling Stanley where to go; and a number of machine learning programs. In total, Stanley's programs contained about 100,000 lines of computer language.

Stanley's driving strategies came from its learning programs. Researchers at Stanford would drive Stanley around. Stanley would record the actions they took, such as turning the wheel or braking, and the sensor input that went with those actions. Then its learning software would try to learn general driving strategies from this input.

According to an article published in Wired magazine, up until three months before the big race Stanley would behave in strange ways. For example, if its sensors wobbled it might think that boulders were causing the wobbling and swerve to avoid them, when it might just be wind. Or it might see a shadow on the road and think the shadow was a ditch. Then the Stanford researchers programmed Stanley to look critically at its sensor input, assigning each little part of the input a sort of "trustworthiness" score and changing its behavior only if it trusted itself. Suddenly, Stanley began to drive more predictably and accurately.

So, Stanley won the 2005 Grand Challenge by using perception, action, and learning. The two CMU vehicles, which came second and third in the race, used similar ways of perceiving and acting, but a different approach to learning. CMU team people spent 28 days driving in the desert, covering 2000 miles and building a detailed electronic map of the desert. They satellite images of the desert and human input about boulders, fence posts, and ditches along the race course. Their approach relied heavily on knowledge representation. In the end, though, only 2% of the actual race course was on their maps.

Figure 8.3: Urban Challenge 2007. One of these cars is driving itself; the others are driven by humans.

The 2007 Challenge was the first Urban Challenge. Eleven vehicles were selected. The race course covered 60 miles on an air force base in California. The prize was $2,000,000. In addition to distance and time rules, the vehicles hand to obey traffic rules and not crash into each other. Six teams finished this race. As with the 2005 Grand Challenge, the top two teams came from CMU and Stanford. Interestingly, two of the vehicles in the top six were hybrid cars.

Although the 2005 and 2007 Challenges were successes, the fastest car in the 2007 Urban Challenge only went 14 miles per hour. By now many cars you can buy have limited perceiving and acting abilities. For example, some models of the Lexus basically park themselves.

8.4 Learning: Computers Rating Products

Today, many people post on the World Wide Web ratings or reviews of things they buy. For example, if you buy a book from Amazon you can read reviews of that book. There are also sites, such as Epinions and Rotten Tomatoes, that contain only reviews. What if a computer could read the text of reviews and other "opinion" statements, and then summarize all that information into a single rating for you?

Ellen Spertus, then a student at Massachusetts Institute of Technology and now a professor at Mills College, was one of the first people to look at whether computers could learn about the opinions or emotions of people from what they write. She looked at postings to newsgroups, which are similar to today's discussion boards. Her program analyzed the words in the postings, for example finding putdowns such as "you bozos" or insults such as "stink". Then, by using a type of machine learning called "decision tree induction," her program separated the postings into two groups: flame and not-flame.

Figure 8.4: *Turing test*

Soon, people were using text analysis and machine learning for all types of tasks, including filtering of spam emails and grouping newspaper stories by topic. However, usually the decision was about a fact: is this news story about a movie? or is this email a spam? People's opinions are much less clear. If I say, *"Charlotte's Web* was interesting but carelessly written" do I mean that I liked it, that I thought it was okay, or that I hated it? Now that there are thousands of book, computer, camera, shampoo, and other product reviews on the World Wide Web, more and more people are trying to sort and classify them.

Bo Pang, a student at Cornell, has used machine learning to automatically decide whether a movie review is positive or negative. She used over 100 movie reviews, from which she took all the words and all word pairs in order. She used several different machine learning methods. Her system decided right about 83% of the time. A system like this one could be used to build an automatic version of the site Rotten Tomatoes, so that you could decide which movie to go see.

Of course, machine learning is also used for other things. In fact, machine learning is used with automatic perception to help self-driving cars decide how to drive and with text processing to help computers learn and use chemistry facts.

8.5 When Do Computers Become Smart?

AI has a big problem. We don't know when we can say that a computer is "smart". For example, spam filters use many of the techniques and methods of AI, but are spam filters "smart"?

Sidebar

In some situations, it can be quite easy for a computer program to pass the Turing test, as long as the "examiner" is not told that she might be talking with a computer. For example, the program Eliza (created in 1966 by Joseph Weizenbaum) fooled humans into thinking they were talking with a psychologist. This does not prove that computers are smart, just that humans are trusting (or gullible!). Or maybe that people expect psychologists to sometimes talk in strange ways.

  To talk to Eliza, go to `http://nlp-addiction.com/eliza/`.

In 1950, Alan Turing, a famous computer scientist, designed a test for telling whether a computer is smart. In his test, a computer and a person are put in different rooms. Another person, an "examiner", sits in a third room. He talks with both the computer and the person using a sort of chat interface and tries to guess which is which. If he can't tell the person from the computer, then the computer passes the test.

Interestingly, Turing predicted that 50 years after he proposed the test, computers would be able to pass the test. That would have been in the year 2000! In 1990, a gold medal and a $100,000 prize, the Loebner Prize, was offered for the first program that can pass the test, and a contest is held every year with a $2,000 prize for the best program of that year. So far no program has won the $100,000 prize.

The 2005 contest was won by Rolly Carpenter and his program called Jabberwacky. You can see part of the conversations with some of the contestants, including Jabberwacky, at `http://loebner.net/Prizef/2005_Contest/Transcripts.html`. Jabberwacky is actually on-line twenty-four hours a day. If you want to talk with it, go to `http://www.jabberwacky.com`. The 2007 contest was won by Robert Medeksza, who has a program called Hal that can act as "your digital secretary and companion". You can try it out online at `http://zabaware.com`.

The Turing test might not test real "smarts". Is intelligence really the ability to carry on a conversation? What about very smart people like Doug Engelbart, the inventor of the mouse, who can create all sorts of new things but have a hard time explaining them to other people? What about other types of intelligence, such as common sense, or street smarts, or the intelligence a cat has that lets it catch a mouse, or the driving skills of Stanley the car? How about human feelings, such as a mother has for her child?

Raymond Kurzweil, a technologist, has predicted that artificial intelligence will continue to seem pretty "dumb" to humans for a little while, but that actually computers are becoming exponentially smarter. One day, he says, there will be a "technological singularity" after which computers will become much smarter than humans. This prediction causes some people to worry that humans might become unnecessary or that

---

Sidebar

Computers that can pass the Turing Test have been the subject of many science fiction books and movies. One of the earliest such computers is HAL-9000 from the 1968 movie 2001: A Space Odyssey, which was re-released in 2001 and is still widely available on DVD. The author of the novel for the movie, Arthur Clarke, said that the name HAL stands for Heuristically programmed ALgorithmic computer. But many people have noted that each of the letters in HAL just happens to occur in the alphabet directly before the letters in IBM. No matter what the name stands for, HAL is a computer that controls a space ship and converses with the crew in a way that would certainly pass the Turing Test. Interestingly, HAL beats one of the astronauts in a game of chess. Unfortunately, later in the movie, HAL has a "nervous breakdown" and almost destroys the space ship.

Computer-driven robots in more modern science fiction movies and TV shows, such as Commander Data in Star Trek and R2D2 in Star Wars, can pass the Turing test, but turn out to be harmless and in fact helpful to the people with which they interact. But sometimes they get into a bit of trouble because they don't have the same kind of feelings that people do.

---

smart computers might treat us as slaves, as in the movie "The Matrix". However, AI researchers focus on smart computers that *help* people, not that would *replace* people.

But all of this research (in AI and other computer science areas) brings up some intriguing philosophical, ethical, and legal issues about what we will allow computers to do – no matter how artificially intelligent they might become

- What makes a person a human being, as distinguished from a computer?

  - What about judgment, life-experience, street smarts, conscience, feelings, empathy, love? Some might ask about an appreciation of music or of a beautiful sunset.

- What kinds of tasks will we allow a computer to do, even after we can write programs to do them?

  - Would we allow a computer to make a decision that might result in someone going to jail? Or being subject to the death penalty?

  - Would we allow a computer to make a medical decision that might result in someone dying?

  - Would we allow a computer to make any decision on which lives depend?

  - Would we let a computer bring up a child? Or be a nanny to a child? Or be a babysitter to a child?

Name: Daphne Koller
Born: 1985
Accomplishment: Winner of a 2004 MacArthur Fellowship

We do already allow computers to make decisions on which people's lives depend. Examples include the control system for the space shuttle; the air traffic control system; and systems that control X-ray and other medical machines.

As computer technology matures and the capabilities of computers increase, these philosophical, legal, and ethical questions will take on increased importance.

8.6 Daphne Koller: Genius of Artificial Intelligence

In 2004, Daphne Koller won a John D. and Catherine T. MacArthur Fellowship. The MacArthur Fellowships, often called the "Genius Awards," are given to people who demonstrate "exceptional creativity, promise for important future advances based on a track record of significant accomplishments, and potential for the fellowship to facilitate subsequent creative work." Each fellow receives $500,000 over five years. The funds come with "no strings attached" so the fellows can use the money as they see fit.

Her Life Daphne Koller was born in Jerusalem, Israel in 1968. In 1985 she received a bachelors degree in mathematics and computer science and in 1986 (at the age of 18) she received a masters degree in computer science, both from the Hebrew University of Jerusalem. She came to the United States on July 4 1989 (Independence Day) to start her Ph.D. at Stanford. In 1993 she received a Ph.D. in computer science from Stanford, where she won the Arthur. L. Samuel award for the best thesis in the Computer Science Department. After spending a two-year post-doc at Berkeley, she returned to Stanford, where she is now an Associate Professor.

She is married to Dan Avida, the CEO of a startup company. They have two children.

What She Accomplished Daphne does some of the best research on computers that learn. Her research is so good because it can be used for so many different things. Just in the last three years, Daphne has applied her work on computers that learn to: understanding human language; helping robots find doors; computer animation; finding genes; and tracking tuberculosis. In fact, her work on robot learning was done with Sebastian Thrun, the team leader for the Stanley car.

One of the biggest problems that Daphne has looked at is how a computer can learn which things it knows about are related, how strongly they are related, and what the relationships between those things are.

Daphne has won several awards for her research, including a Sloan Fellowship in 1996, a Computers and Thought Award in 2001, and a MacArthur Fellowship in 2004.

Stories About Her Daphne's research group of students at Stanford is known as DAGS, Daphne's Approximate Group of Students.

Daphne likes to read, listen to music, and hike. Daphne and Dan like to take vacations to exotic locations, in the Caribbean, Europe, and Asia. On those vacations, they like to hike, sail, and scuba dive.

8.7 Martha Pollack: Famous AI Researcher

Martha Pollack is a computer scientist who has, through her work, affected almost every person working on AI today. She is a fellow, and also President, of the American Association for Artificial Intelligence. In 1991 she won the Computers and Thought Award, a prestigious award for AI researchers.

Her Life Martha Pollack was born and brought up in Stamford, Connecticut. She graduated from Dartmouth College in 1979. Her major was linguistics – an interdisciplinary major she created, because Dartmouth did not have a linguistics department. She also took as many math courses as a math major. She got her Masters and Ph.D. degrees in Computer and Information Science from the University of Pennsylvania in 1984 and 1986. She won the Rubinoff Dissertation Prize for her Ph.D. dissertation.

Martha worked as a researcher for SRI International from 1986 to 1991, and then as a professor at the University of Pittsburgh until 2000.

Name: Martha Pollack
Born: 1958
Accomplishment: Winner, Computers and Thought Award

She then moved to the University of Michigan where she was the only female professor in the Computer Science and Engineering Division. She ended up chairing that division from 2004-2007, and then became Dean of the School of Information.

Martha is married and has two children and two cats.

What She Accomplished   Martha's research is on computers that can plan. Giving computers the ability to plan (or think ahead) is important because computers can use that ability to help humans.

For example, Martha worked on the robot Pearl that can help elderly and disabled people manage their lives. By reasoning about these people's plans, it can remind them to eat, drink, take their medicine, or use the bathroom. It can also guide them from room to room and chat about the weather or TV listings. In 2004 Martha testified before congress on technology to support older adults.

When Martha was awarded the Computers and Thought Award in 1991, she was the first woman to receive it. In 1996 she was elected a fellow of the American Association of Artificial Intelligence. More recently, she received the Sarah Goddard Power award in recognition of her work to increase the number of women in science and engineering.

Martha has organized AI conferences and been on the editorial boards of all the important AI journals. She is also an excellent teacher. She has won several teaching awards and her students have won awards for their scientific papers. In fact, she is most proud of her students' awards.

Chapter 9

Human-Computer Interaction

9.1 What is HCI?

In the previous chapters, we have looked at various things that go on *inside* a computer: how it is built, how it is programmed, what it can do, what it cannot do. However, computers don't just sit all by themselves and calculate. Computers are all around us. In fact, you probably wear or carry at least three computers with you each day – your music player, your cell phone, and a laptop or portable gaming system.

While some computers (such as those in your car) pretty much operate independently of humans, many interact with humans through an interface. In other words, humans and computers inhabit a shared world. Human-Computer Interaction, or HCI, is the study of the range of interactions between humans and computers. Some HCI experts design user interfaces for existing computers that are (hopefully) efficient and user-friendly. Others invent new devices for human-computer interaction (for example, pens instead of mice, and speech input instead of typing on a keyboard). Still others look at new ways in which humans can interact with computers; for example, groups of humans (instead of a single human) interacting with a computer.

In this chapter, we will first look at some design guidelines for user interfaces. Then we will look at some unusual types of interface. Finally, we will describe some new approaches to HCI.

9.2 Designing User Interfaces

A user interface is any kind of way for a human to provide input to a computer, or for a computer to provide output to a human. For example,

Figure 9.1: *Douglas Engelbart's Interface*

the user interface to an MP3 player is the screen that shows the song being played and the buttons and menus that let a user choose a song. Even very small and simple devices, such as digital thermometers and watches, now have screen-and-button interfaces. On the other hand, personal computers that are useful for many tasks now have complex graphical user interfaces (GUIs) and let you provide input in many ways, including keyboard, mouse, pen, and speech.

The first person to describe an interface resembling the modern GUI was Vannevar Bush, then at MIT. He did this in the 1930's, before there were even any commercial computers! His idea was a device called the Memex that would have a GUI interface and touch-screen displays. The Memex would be able to access "all the knowledge in the world," which would be stored on microfilm and be accessed using links very much like those used on the World Wide Web.

In the late 1940's, Douglas Engelbart, at Stanford Research Institute, read an article by Bush and decided to try to create a machine that would, in his words, "augment human intellect." In 1968, he demonstrated his technology: an early windowing interface, with two types of keyboard and a type of mouse. During the 1970's these ideas were further developed by Xerox. The first commercially available computer with this type of interface was the Xerox Star 8010, which was announced in 1981. Shortly after that, Apple released the Lisa and Macintosh computers and Microsoft released Windows 1.0, all of which used a similar interface. Now most personal computers have a GUI interface. This type of GUI is called a WIMP (windows, icon, menu, pointing device).

WIMP-based GUIs have many advantages. For example, they are easy to learn and to use. However, people have also experimented with other types of GUI. For example, Microsoft Bob was a story-telling interface for Microsoft products that was developed in the 1990's by a team led by

---

Sidebar

You have used many devices in your life that might not seem to be computers or to have interfaces. For example, maybe you have flown on an airplane and used the in-seat controls for the television, music, and lights. Maybe you have a digital camera. Or maybe you had some electronic toys when you were little.

Think of some devices you have used. If you are having trouble, go to any store and look around. Once you have a list of devices, pick one that had the best interface and one that had the worst. (The bad ones are probably easier to remember!) What made the interaction with the bad one so bad? What was so great about the interaction with the good one?

Melinda Gates (then Melinda French). Many computer games also have story-telling interfaces that use text, audio, graphics, and a joystick.

Project Looking Glass is another example of an innovative type of GUI. Like most GUIs today, it uses windows, a keyboard, and a mouse. However, windows in this GUI can be treated like 3-dimensional objects. For example, you can turn them around and write on their backs.

Up until the early 1990's, if you wanted to design a user interface you had to be a really good programmer. Now, anyone can create a user interface using special interface design programs. Although anyone can create a user interface, this does not mean that everyone will create good user interfaces. We have all had experience with bad user interfaces, so obviously making a good interface is not as easy as it might seem.

Some HCI experts have spent their lives studying what makes a good user interface. Here are five sample guidelines borrowed from Don Norman, the author of *The Design of Everyday Things*:

- Visibility – The key functionalities of the software should be visible in the interface.

- Feedback – The user should be given timely feedback about the results of every action taken in the interface. For example, if the user creates a new file in Windows, that file is immediately visible.

- Consistency – Interfaces should be internally consistent and consistent with each other. For example, the keyboard shortcuts in many Windows applications are the same.

- User control – The user should be given as much control as possible. For example, many interfaces provide keyboard shortcuts as well as menus.

- Error prevention and recovery – Identify functionalities where the user might make important errors. Check with the user before executing these functionalities. Give helpful error messages. Provide an undo when possible.

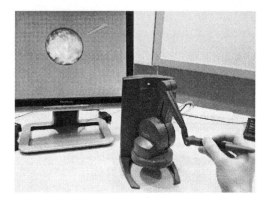

Figure 9.2: *Another kind of unusual interface. This Sensable device is like a 3D mouse.*

Also, the design of a user interface should be tuned to the capabilities of the expected users of that interface and the context in which that interface will be used. For example, the eBay Web page and the interface to an ATM are quite simple and intuitive and can be used by almost anyone without the need for a user manual. The interface used by an airline reservations clerk is much more complicated (partly because the task the clerk is doing is more complicated) and requires some training and a user manual before it can be effectively used.

9.3   Unusual User Interfaces

The GUI is the standard user interface for personal computers. However, there are many other types of user interface for small devices, special tasks, or particular types of user. Let's look at some examples.

Telesurgery is long-distance surgery. The surgeon sits at a computer. The screen shows video of the patient on the operating table. Attached to the computer are mechanical arms that control surgical instruments in the operating room, which can be far away from where the surgeon is sitting. The surgeon moves these arms to perform the surgery and can see the effect of his motions on the screen. The world's first telesurgery was performed on September 7, 2001. A doctor in New York removed the gallbladder of a patient in Strasbourg, France.

Stephen Hawking is a world-famous physicist and author. He is also a sufferer from ALS (Amytropic Lateral Sclerosis), which leaves him virtually completely paralyzed.. He uses a computer interface to communicate with the world. On his wheelchair, he has a computer with a GUI and a switch (similar to a mouse button). Using only this switch and specialized software (including a text-to-speech synthesizer and a dictionary application), he is able to control the lights and doors in his home, lecture in public, write papers and books, and talk on the telephone.

Figure 9.3: *The I/O Brush*

Kimiko Ryokai, a researcher at the MIT Media Lab, has invented a special electronic paint brush, the I/O brush. It looks like an ordinary paint brush, but it contains a little camera. When held over a surface, it takes a picture of that surface. Then, on a special canvas, you can paint with the picture as your "color." Picture 9.3 shows the I/O brush being used by children. Kimiko says that with the I/O brush, "you are no longer pointing and shooting and thinking about capturing the environment, but using the environment to create something very new."

The Nintendo Wii and the iPhone are two commercial products with unusual user interfaces. The iPhone has a touch screen instead of a keyboard. The Wii has a 3D controller that gives users much more freedom than a mouse or joystick.

9.4 New Types of HCI

Most of us are now used to using computers as tools and as entertainment devices. However, these activities are essentially one-on-one: one user, one computer. Also, the computer is usually the assistant and the human is usually "in charge." In this section, we will look at two different types of human-computer interaction: one in which the user and computer are engaged in a full-body dialog, and one in which multiple users and one or more computers complete a task together.

REA, the Real Estate Agent, is an *embodied conversational agent* that can recommend houses and give virtual tours. Humans provide input to REA using speech and hand gestures. REA provides output on a screen, both as a "virtual human" who can talk and gesture back at the human, and in the form of pictures of houses. REA's body is the same size as

Figure 9.4: *A Second Life persona. How many of the other players in on-line games or environments are really computer programs, not humans?*

an adult's body and REA uses the same types of interaction as a human does (speech and gesture). So you can't really say the user "uses" REA; rather, the user has a dialog with REA. REA was developed by Justine Cassell, whose biography is in the next section.

Sometimes computers serve as a support for human-human inter-action. Examples include blogs, wikis, multiplayer online games and virtual worlds. Blogs and wikis are mostly text-based, while most multi-player online games and virtual worlds like Second Life permit multime-dia interaction. Many-user multimedia online environments like Second Life have inspired computer scientists in many fields other than HCI, including networking, security and database research.

In multiplayer games and chat rooms, some players are computer programs rather than humans. An early example of such a program is Cobot. Cobot was a computer program that lived in a virtual world, LambdaMOO, visited by hundreds of people every day. Cobot could in-troduce people who were in the same "room" in the LambdaMOO. It also kept track of which visitors to the LambdaMOO had talked to each other and what they had said. Over time, it became able to tell visitors who their friends were. Finally, Cobot could chat in a general way with visi-tors to the LambdaMOO.

Researchers are working on computer programs that will travel around with their "owners" in the real world and keep track of who they meet and what they do. For example, there is now software you can download on your cellphone that you can use to find out where your friends are, or even to be told when there is someone located near you who might like to ask you out. These programs have the potential to significantly change human-human interaction, making it more like online interaction.

Name: Justine Cassell
Born: 1960
Accomplishment: Creator of Embodied Conversational Agents

9.5 Justine Cassell: Creator of Embodied Conversational Agents

Her Life   Justine Cassell was born in New York City in 1960. She says

> I was born pretty much a word person. I was asking questions
> about words even as I was learning how to talk. By the time I
> was seven or eight, I kept a wordbook in which I would write
> good words. My parents would say, "Now why is that a good
> word?" and I would say, "It just is." One of them was "sphyg-
> momanometer," what they take your blood pressure with. I
> loved writing and I stayed up all night and read novels trying
> to finish them in one night.

Justine's education was very unusual and a is lesson in the power of
determination. She started college at Dartmouth. She says

> I kept taking biology, chemistry, and math and doing badly in
> them. I also kept taking English and comparative literature and
> doing well in them. Then in my sophomore year, I took a course
> on the history of the English language and I realized that what
> I loved was the history of the language. I loved especially how
> children learn language.

While she was a student at Dartmouth, Justine spent two years at the
University of Besancon in France studying linguistics. She received un-
dergraduate degrees from the University of Besancon in 1981 and from
Dartmouth in 1982.

Justine next entered the Master's program in linguistics at the University of Edinburgh. She says

> When I arrived and told them that I wanted to look at the lin-
> guistics of literary texts on the one hand, and of children's lan-

guage on the other hand, they very quickly said, "That's not linguistics."

Nonetheless, for her Master's thesis, she researched how children learn to tell stories.

After her time at Edinburgh, Justine entered the Ph.D. program in psychology at the University of Chicago. She says

As soon as I arrived, I told them I wanted to continue my work in looking at how children learn how to become storytellers, and they very quickly told me that was not psychology. I decided that what I needed to do was get a Ph.D. in both linguistics and psychology. That way, no one could tell me that I wasn't one of them.

Justine received her double Ph.D. in linguistics and psychology from the University of Chicago in 1991. However, she had already started working as an Assistant Professor at Pennsylvania State University in three separate departments, the Departments of Linguistics, Psychology, and French. In 1994 she left Pennsylvania State University and spent a year a National Science Foundation Visiting Professor at the University of Pennsylvania in the Department of Computer Science and the Institute for Research in Cognitive Science. In 1995, she joined the Media Lab at MIT (first as an Assistant Professor and then as an Associate Professor) where she directed the Gesture and Narrative Language Research Group. In 2004, she left MIT to become a Full Professor at Northwestern University where she has joint appointments in Computer Science and Communication Studies and is director of the interdisciplinary graduate program in Technology and Social Behavior.

What She Accomplished   Justine has more than 70 publications, including the book she co-edited called "From Barbie to Mortal Kombat: Gender and Computer Games". Because of the innovative nature of her research, she has won several awards (such as the Edgerton Faculty Achievement Award at MIT) and has repeatedly been invited to give talks to other researchers and to the public (for example, by PBS). In addition to her scientific research, she has conducted research on women in academia, minorities in education, and children's education. This research has led to several outreach activities. To give just one example, Justine founded the Junior Summit, a program to bring children from different countries together to discuss how technology could help them.

In 2008 Justine was given the Women of Vision Leadership Award by the Anita Borg Institute of Women and Technology.

Stories About Her   As we have said, Justine is very interested in the education of children and in their interactions with computers.

Figure 9.5: *Justine with one of the conversational agents she has created.*

- In commenting on games that are meant to attract girls to computers, she said that designing games "specially for girls" risks highlighting girls as a population that needs "special help" in their relation to technology

   > *My students and I ... didn't see that it was our place to design a game for girls or a game for boys. We didn't see that it was our place to claim to know what girl was or what boy was, because there was too much diversity. So we decided to design computer games that in their way would allow children to decide who they were, and to discover who they were in the richest way we could. I call this design philosophy undetermined design.*

   In 1998, Justine was co-editor, with Henry Jenkins, of the book "From Barbie to Mortal Kombat: Gender and Computer Games," which addresses these issues.

- In 1998, Justine organized and directed a project for children around the world called Junior Summit. It gathered over 3,000 children from 149 different countries online. The project handed out computers and online connections. The goal was "to give voice to girls, to children from developing nations, to all people, in both a metaphoric and concrete sense." 100 of these children participated in a 5-day summit in Boston, where they promoted their ideas to world leaders and the international press.

Some advice she has given for girls and women who are beginning to learn about computers and technology:

- Don't take anything for granted and don't think you have to fit into the status quo to succeed.

- If you feel that you can make computers or technology do something totally different, then go for it.

- So many young women tell me that, even though they love technology, they don't "see themselves" in Computer Science. I reply: make Computer Science LOOK LIKE YOU.

- Two pieces of advice for girls and women who are just starting: YOU CAN'T BREAK IT and MAKE IT YOURS.

Chapter 10

Amanda Builds a Computer

I had been a computer scientist for years, but had never built a computer. To be honest, I felt like I had been cheated! Then my husband, Liam, showed me how. In this chapter, we will describe how to build a personal computer. We will show pictures of the computer we built for a friend, who was upgrading from a 500 MHZ computer with a 128 MB of RAM and a 13 GB hard drive. Our friend's computer was quite a bit out-of-date, and, as you will see, the computer we built is much faster and has more memory.

What do all those numbers mean?

- *A 500 MHZ (megahertz) computer* describes how fast the computer computes. One of the parts of the computer is its processor (also called its CPU or central processing unit). The processor is the "brain" of the computer and performs the machine language instructions we want the computer to execute. Inside the processor is a clock that synchronizes its operations. 500 MHZ refers to how fast that clock ticks – in this case 500 million times per second.

- *128 MB (megabytes) of RAM* describes how much random access memory the computer has. Any location in random access memory can be accessed in one step using its address. Addresses in RAMs are just numbers, 0, 1, 2, ... So we can retrieve from a RAM the information stored at address 567, in the same amount of time it would take to retrieve the information stored at address 567000. RAMs are volatile storage, meaning that when the computer is turned off, all the data stored in the RAM is lost.

  A megabyte is a million bytes. A byte is eight bits and can store one character – for example the letter **q** or the numeral **8**. So the RAM in our friend's computer could store 128 million characters. This chapter of this book contains about 30 thousand characters.

Sidebar

Recall that one of the sidebars in Section 2.2.2 quoted a predication that Bill Gates, the President of Microsoft, made in 1981:

640K (of memory) ought to be enough for anybody.

640K means 640 thousand. So the 128 million bytes of RAM of our friend's outdated computer was already 200 times larger than that prediction.

As you will see, the computer we built for our friend has 1 GB (gigabyte) of RAM. A gigabyte is a thousand million bytes, so the RAM of the computer we built is more than 1000 times larger than Bill Gates's prediction. This much RAM is fine for our friend, who writes books and surfs the internet. Liam has 8 GB of RAM in his computer. If you play a lot of computer games or watch videos on your computer you need more RAM than if you don't.

- *A 13 GB (gigabyte) hard drive (disk)* describes how much information can be stored on the hard drive. The hard drive is persistent storage. This means that the information stored on the hard drive is not lost when the computer is turned off. But it takes a relatively long time to retrieve information from a hard drive, because the information is stored magnetically on disks (little flat dishes or platters). You have to wait until the disk spins around far enough for you to read the information you want from the disk.

  A gigabyte is a thousand million bytes of information, so even the relatively small hard drive on our friend's outdated computer could store a large amount of information. By comparison, this entire book, including the figures, contains about 40 million bytes.

Hard drives are used to store the instructions and data for all the programs the computer might want to execute. When the user wants to execute a program, the instructions and data for that program are copied from the hard drive into the RAM, where it can be retrieved faster. Then the instructions in the program are brought one at a time from the RAM into the processor where they are executed. The machine language instructions that the processor can execute are very simple, for example:

- Fetch the data stored at a particular address in the RAM into the processor and add it to some other data that is already stored in the processor.

- Store a piece of data that is stored in the processor into some address in the RAM.

- Display on the screen some data that is stored in the processor.

As we explained in Section 3.2, compilers are used to translate a program written in a high-level language such as Java or C++ into the machine language instructions of the computer on which it is to be executed – more precisely into the machine language instructions of the processor in that computer.

How do you build a computer? Building a computer today is quite easy. This is because we can buy the parts (such as the processor, hard drive and RAM) already built. All we have to do is assemble them. We can also buy other pre-built components such as a sound card, which produces the sounds we want to hear, and a video card, which produces the pictures on our screen.

One other part we can buy is the motherboard. The motherboard contains all the wiring to connect the other parts and sockets into which those other parts can by plugged. The part of the motherboard that includes this wiring and the sockets is called the bus. Thus building the computer consists mostly of plugging the parts we bought into the appropriate sockets on the motherboard.

Interestingly, in our multi-national world, the individual parts might have been manufactured in many different countries all around the world, but they can all be assembled together because they are built to match the same standards.

10.1 The Ingredients

Even though assembling the computer is simple, there are a lot of choices involved. You can't just go to the store and buy "the standard" equipment. You have to know what you want.

First, choose a computer processor or chip; for example, an Intel or AMD chip. Think about the speed you want, the type of operating system you want to install (Windows, Linux, OS X), and the kind of case you want to house the computer in. If you will be playing lots of computer games, for example, you want a faster processor. If all you are doing is word processing and Web browsing, you can buy a slower processor. My friend uses the Web and does quite a bit of word processing, but that's about it, so we bought him a Celeron 2.53 GHz (gigahertz) chip.

Second, choose a case. You can buy one on the internet or at a good computer store. Since the case often includes a motherboard, you must choose a case that says it matches the chip you have chosen and that will support the peripherals (hard drives, DVD/CD burners, etc) and cards (video, sound, modem) you will use. Be sure to read the description of the case carefully – some cases come with motherboards, fans, even sound cards already in them. We bought an ASUS case (ASUS is the brand name), which is inexpensive but includes a motherboard, a 3.5 inch floppy drive, and space for a DVD/CD player – the two things my friend asked for. It even has an FM radio receiver – a nice bonus!

Third, choose the other things that will go in your case, such as:

- Motherboard – if your case does not come with one, you may need to buy a motherboard to hold all these cards and your chip. Buy one that says it fits your chip.

Figure 10.1: *Parts for our computer*

Figure 10.2: *Our computer's case*

- Memory – you will want more RAM than the minimum required for your chip, but probably not the maximum it or your motherboard can support (at least to start with). RAM is still one of the most expensive parts of the computer after the chip.

- Sound card – choose a nice one if you have a big MP3 collection or play games.

- Video card – choose a fancy one if you play lots of games or watch TV on your computer.

- Modem – if you use dial-up internet access.

- Hard drive – you can get a truly huge hard drive today, but you may not need it unless you are storing lots of images, movies, and music on it.

- DVD/CD player or burner – A DVD player will also play CDs so you don't need both. (The word "burner" just refers to the ability to record a DVD or CD.)

- Fan/power supply – if your case or your chip do not come with these, you should buy ones that match your chip.

For our computer, we bought a fan for the chip, 1 GB of RAM, a modem, an 80 GB hard drive, and a multi-format DVD burner. However, we later discovered that the case came with a fan for the chip (we should have read the case contents more carefully!).

Picture 10.1 shows the parts we bought, and picture 10.2 shows the case and the things that came with it. Many cases come with an instruction booklet that walk you step-by-step through building your computer.

Picture 10.3 shows me looking at the back of the computer. You can see the color-coded ports for keyboard, mouse etc. You can also see where the fan blows out the air. And you can see, next to my left thumb, two stenciled parts of the case – we'll get to them later.

10.2 The Recipe

10.2.1 Get your bearings

Okay, now that we had our parts, we had to open the case. The two other things you will need to build a computer are a slotted and a Phillips screwdriver (I call these 'flat' and 'cross' shaped screwdrivers). We unscrewed the cover of the case and took it off. Picture 10.4 shows the inside of the case. The big metal thing in the middle on the bottom is the power supply. The drives go in the metal holder on the top left; the case came with a 3.5 inch floppy drive. You can also see two blue plastic

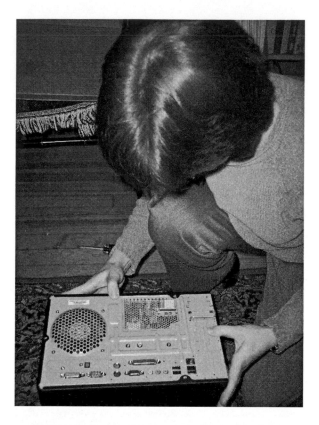

Figure 10.3: *The back of the case (and the back of my head)*

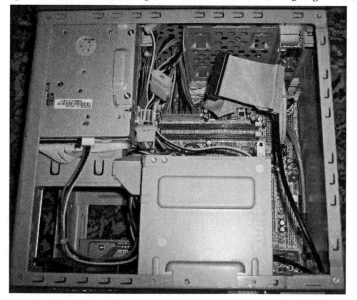

Figure 10.4: *The inside of the case*

Figure 10.5: *The inside of the case without the power supply*

pieces in the upper middle; they are the holders for the memory, and they are on the motherboard, which looks orange in the picture.

Now, the inside of a computer may seem scary at first. Look at all the weird plastic and metal things sticking up and all the wires going everywhere! Here is an important thing to remember: it is very hard to break the computer. You can't break it by touching it, for instance. You can't break it by breathing on it. Nothing bad will happen if you follow the instructions in the manual that comes with the case.

Picture 10.5 shows the inside of the case after we removed the power supply (which we had to unscrew and sort of wiggle out, after unplugging it from the motherboard and floppy drive). Now you can see the fan (it is the black box on the lower right). You can also see, right in the middle, where the chip goes. And you can see the circuitry on the motherboard – all those tiny gray lines, which let the various parts of the computer that are attached to the motherboard talk to each other.

10.2.2 Put in the chip

To install the chip, we unhooked the little metal hook you can see in Picture 10.5 and took out the little piece of plastic under it. Then we took the chip out of its packaging, and held it by its edges (like you'd hold a CD) with the little gold dots facing up so we could find the notches on each side. Then we turned it over and fit it into the holder by its notches. We folded down the metal cover and rehooked the hook. Picture 10.6 shows the chip with the metal dots facing up; the chip in the holder, face down; and the chip holder rehooked.

There is a bit of tricky work to be done on the chip after it is in place.

Figure 10.6: *Putting in the chip: the underside of the chip, the chip in the holder, the chip with the metal cover on*

Figure 10.7: *Putting thermal grease on the chip*

Modern chips produce lots of heat. So a fan sits right on top of the chip, dispersing the heat. To make the fan disperse the heat better, a little bit of "thermal compound" or "heat-sink grease" must be dabbed on top of the chip. The compound comes in a little syringe with the chip or with the case, or you can buy it separately. It is gray, and you **do not** want to get it on your skin or in your eyes or mouth. Just unscrew the top of the syringe, and then touch the syringe to the chip and make 16 or so little dots of grease all over the chip surface (a little goes a long way!). Then, hold the chip's fan on top of the chip and screw it in.

Picture 10.7 shows the syringe and the grease on the chip. Near the chip, you can see the four screw holes where the screws for the chip's fan go. Picture 10.8 shows me screwing in the fan that sits on top of the chip. This particular fan came with the case. A different fan came with the chip, and we had a third fan for the chip just in case (but obviously, we didn't need it!).

10.2.3   Put in the RAM

At this point the computer has no RAM and no hard drive (almost no place to store things). RAM comes as one or more DIMMs (Dual Inline Memory Modules), which are small circuit boards that contain memory chips. DIMMs look like very thin chocolate bars. They have a skinny bit along one side, which is usually in two sections. You hold the DIMM so the skinny bit is facing down, and so the shorter section fits into the shorter section on the "RAM socket" (RAM holder). Then you push. As you can see in Picture 10.9, you might have to push quite hard. Typically there will be a little white bit at each end of the RAM socket. Push gently on the white bit before inserting the RAM, and then, as you push down on the RAM, the white bit will snap or come back up. That's when you know the RAM is fixed in place.

Figure 10.8: Screwing in the chip's fan

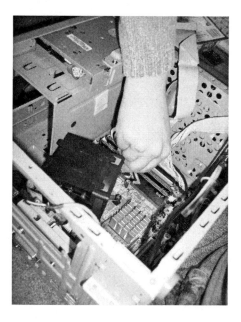

Figure 10.9: Inserting RAM

Figure 10.10: *Screwing the hard drive into its holder*

10.2.4 Put in the hard drive

If you look back at Picture 10.5, at the upper left, just under where
the hand is, you can see two bits of metal sticking out. They are the
sides of the holder for the main hard drive (you can have more than one
hard drive; any others would go in the metal holder on the bottom left
of Picture 10.5). We took the hard drive holder out by pulling up on it,
and then we screwed in the hard drive (Picture 10.10) and put the holder
back (Picture 10.11). You really can't do this wrong. The hard drive is in
a case, which you can touch, and you will find that the holes in the hard
drive line up only one way with those in the holder.

Our hard drive was a type called a "Serial ATA drive" (ATA stands for
Advanced Technology Attachment and describes how the data is transferred to and from the disk). We connected the hard drive to the motherboard using the red cable shown. Most cables in the computer plug
in only one way. Some have a little imprint on them with, say, a "1"
that you can match to a "1" on the place the cable connects. Some have
a pattern of pins that you can match up. Some have a little clip, with
a corresponding clip where the cable is supposed to plug in. You can
check for these signs, or you can look in the manual for the case. (As
the old slogan goes, "If all else fails, read the manual.")

Figure 10.11: The hard drive in the case

10.2.5   Put in the DVD Player

Picture 10.12 shows the case with the front off. You can see the back of the hard drive holder through the holes in the lower half. The DVD player goes in the top half. At the very bottom you can see the places to plug in the microphone and speakers.

To insert the DVD player, we just slid it in through the front of the computer and then screwed it on the side of the case. Then we attached the communication cables to the DVD player. In this case, they were "parallel ATA cables," and you can see them in Picture 10.13. They are gray, with a pink strip at the end, and you plug in the cable so that the pink strip ("pin 1") is lined up with the marking on the player.

You could also add another CD player, another floppy drive, etc., as long as you have room. Of course, you can always use an external drive without adding it to the computer.

10.2.6   Put in the peripherals

Next we inserted the modem. Modems, sound cards, and video cards are all little bits of plastic with gold lines on them (usually the cards themselves are green). To insert a card, first figure out which slot on the motherboard it fits in. Then, punch out the stenciled metal from the part of the case in front of that slot. Hold the card by its edges with the part with the copper connectors facing down, line it up with the slot, and push it firmly in until you hear it click. Finally, screw it into the case where the metal edge lines up with the hole in the case. Picture 10.14 shows me pushing the modem into its slot.

Figure 10.12: The front of the computer

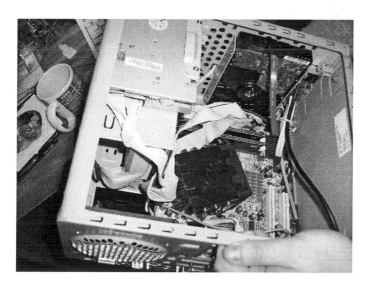

Figure 10.13: The DVD player in the computer

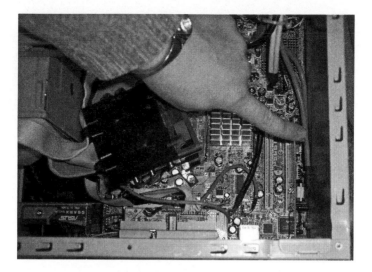

Figure 10.14: Putting in the modem

10.2.7   Hook up the Power

Now, the only thing we had left to do was to replace the power supply. We put the power supply back into the case, and then plugged cables from the power supply into the motherboard (two cables – one for video power and one for auxiliary power), the hard drive, the floppy drive, and the DVD drive. The tricky thing here is not to leave anything out. The power cables all have different sizes, so you just put them where they fit, and make sure they are aligned with the numbers or clips on the sockets into which they go. If you don't plug something in, the computer won't turn on, and then you just fix it. Picture 10.15 shows me plugging a power cable into the floppy drive, and Picture 10.16 shows the power all connected. It looks messy with all those wires running from place to place, but that's okay. You can tuck things in with zip ties if you don't like the messiness. Just keep the cables out of the way of the fans!

At this point, we were done assembling the computer hardware. We put the case cover back on the case and screwed it back in. Picture 10.17 shows the front of the case with all its little doors open so you can see the hardware it has. Picture 10.18 shows the closed case. You would never guess so much had changed inside, would you?

10.3   The Main Meal

What do you think happened when we turned the computer on? Well, we got a very simple text-only interface on the screen that let us set the clock and check if the computer could "see" all the hardware. There were no programs installed yet on the computer.

Figure 10.15: *Plugging a power cable into the floppy drive*

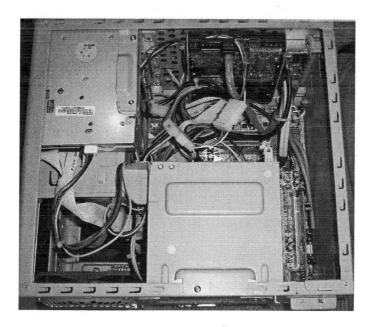

Figure 10.16: *The power supply is back in the computer*

Figure 10.17: *The front of the case*

Figure 10.18: *The finished computer*

Computer hardware executes machine code, but you, the user, get to choose what programs to run on it. So actually, after assembling the computer hardware we were only half done. We had brought with us an operating system (Windows XP), and several programs, including a word processing program. Although my friend hadn't asked for it, we brought him a virus checking program. **This is very important on any computer.** The case and some of the hardware came with other programs, which we also installed. We don't have pictures of these steps because they all look the same. However, these steps were what turned a lovely but useless piece of machinery into a lovely and powerful toy for my friend. Hardware and software are both important, "useless each without the other," as Longfellow said in another context.

Sidebar

You don't have to make a computer that looks like a big gray or black box. There have been some lovely and/or original computer cases. For example, Apple has made computers that looked like toasters, or like flying circles. Another original idea is to do away with the case altogether; see
`http://www.q-news.ch/articles/nhp200nc/`.

Now that you know how to build a computer, draw and list the parts for your own ideal machine. What would the case look like? Would it be clear? Round? Colorful? What kind of processor, memory, and hard drive would you use? What peripherals would you want – an iris scanner, a pen reader, a microphone?

Sidebar

We installed an operating system (Windows XP) on our computer. What is an operating system?

You can think of an operating system as a traffic cop that controls all the traffic inside the computer. You might have thought that a computer is just executing one program at a time. Not true! Right now while I am typing in this chapter using one program on my computer, other programs are also executing in the background, invisibly to me. One, for example, is continually listening to see if I have any email. Another is updating a tiny thermometer on the bottom of my screen with the current temperature. In fact, I just looked and there are a total of 55 programs running right now as I am writing this chapter. I'm not sure what they are all doing, but I'm sure it's something useful (at least I hope so).

Each of these 55 programs needs to use the CPU to execute. But my PC has only one CPU. So one thing the operating system does is to schedule the use of the CPU. It lets each program use the CPU, one at a time, each for a fraction of a second.

Also each program needs to use some RAM, so the operating system assigns some parts of RAM to each program and makes sure it does not use any RAM other than that assigned to it. Once in a while each program wants to read or write to the hard drive, and the operating system manages that. If a program wants to write something on the monitor screen, it tells the operating system what it wants to do and the operating system does it. Every time you type a letter on the keyboard or click on the mouse, the operating system responds to that input and sends it to the correct program.

The operating system does a great many other things as well, but you get the idea. Some people have compared an operating system to a juggler trying to keep all the programs up-in-the-air (running) at the same time.

Don't think that the tasks the operating system does are simple. Just to show you how complicated they can be, the Windows Vista operating system contains more than 50 million lines of code.

Now that I have built my own computer, I find myself even more fascinated by computer science, particularly software. I can think of only one thing in the world that can change the way it operates as much as a computer, and that is a human being.

10.4 Amanda Stent: Computational Linguist

I am a computational linguist, teacher, and researcher. I am also a pianist, voracious reader, and amateur birdwatcher.

My Life. I was born in Sahiwal, Pakistan in 1974. My favorite subject in school was mathematics. However, in 9th grade I was introduced to the AI programming language Prolog, and I "fell in love" with it. (I remember in high school being torn between two projects: building an expert system for looking at criminals, and writing a computer virus for the Amiga, a type of computer. So you see, in your life sometimes you have to choose in which direction to go.) I received a B.A. in mathematics and music from Houghton College in upstate New York in 1996, and a Ph.D. in Computer Science from the University of Rochester (specializing in artificial intelligence) in 2001. My favorite year of college was my junior year, which I spent in Scotland, at the University of Edinburgh, studying computer science.

I have worked at Eastman Kodak Corporation, AT&T Research Labs, and Stony Brook University. I do research on spoken dialog systems, which are computer programs that communicate with humans using speech. I have published almost 40 research papers and hold one patent. I have done research projects with nine undergraduates and many graduate students. In fall 2006, I got married to one of the smartest people I know, who is also a 'computer person'.

I like doing new things. In 2005 I bought a house, took up all the carpet, and laid down wooden flooring myself. This meant I had to learn to use a table saw, which was very exciting. Recently, I have become interested in standup comedy and in particular how people communicate "funny" by using their tone of voice and pauses in their speech. Maybe I will do some research on this subject so that I can understand it better.

Stories. There is one thing that makes me more excited than anything else, and that is understanding something. One day I told a friend about a magic trick my father used to play, in which he would pull a coin out from behind your ear. I could never figure out how he did it. My friend said, "Perhaps it's an act of God". My response was, "I can't accept that, I'm a scientist".

I don't like being told that I can't or shouldn't do something because I am a woman. I don't think women need extra help to be computer scientists – each person has their own skills. In my small high school, I was told by a teacher that I should not do well in mathematics-oriented classes, so that my brother would not be forced to compete with me and so that he could perform better. I got A's in all my math and computer science classes. My brother did fine and today is a computer engineer.

In my first year at college, I was a music major. At the end of that year, I went to my advisor because I was thinking of switching to mathematics. When my advisor asked why, I said that I didn't think I was a good enough musician to earn a living teaching or performing. My advisor said, "But music is very good preparation for being a housewife". By the following semester, I had switched my major and my advisor.

I consider computer science to be an ideal career because it is flexible and exciting. A computer scientist can be a "people person" or an "idea person"; a scientist, engineer, or artist; a traveler, or a homebody. In addition to understanding the computer itself, computer science helps me understand how problems can be solved and how people communicate with each other. And in computer science you will always be surprised, always have more to learn and more to do. I also like computer science because so many computer scientists have lived in other countries. This means that in the workplace I get to experience all sorts of different cultures and perspectives.

Chapter 11

Just the FAQs

The acronym FAQ is short for *frequently asked question.* In this chapter we will answer some frequently asked questions about computer science as a career: how to become a computer scientist, being a computer scientist, and what a computer scientist does in her spare time.

For more information about women in computer science, take a minute to check out our website at www.theprincessatthekeyboard.com.

11.1 Becoming a Computer Scientist

11.1.1 How do I find out if I am interested in computer science?

By reading this book you have made a good start! Here are some other ideas:

- Contact the nearest college university and ask if they have any programs to support high school students interested in computer science, such as WISE (Women in Science and Engineering) program, Intel summer research, or a summer program for high school students interested in computer science.

- Look on the internet for summer camps or summer courses in computer science or special topics, such as robotics.

- Take a course in computer science in high school. Only 21,113 students took AP Computer Science in 2007, and only 17% of those students were women. If you take a computer science class in your high school, you will get individualized attention and a head start on computer science.

- Find out if there is a computer club at your school and join it.

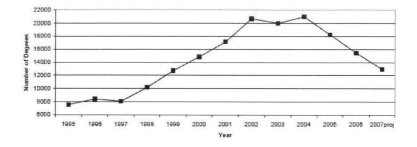

Figure 11.1: *Bachelor's degrees in computer science over time, as reported by the Computing Research A*

- Ask if you can shadow a computer scientist at work at a local company or university.

11.1.2   If I am interested in computer science, will that scare all the guys away?

Our answer to that question is another question:

> *Why would you want to be friends with any guy who is scared off by the fact that you are a smart girl who is interested in computer science?*

There are plenty of smart guys who want to be friends with smart girls. And many of them are interested in computer science themselves.

11.1.3   How many people do a computer science major in college?

The number changes a lot, since the number of people who choose to major in computer science seems to follow the state of the economy. According to the Digest of Education Statistics, in 2003-04 59,488 people received Bachelor's degrees in computer and information sciences, while in 2005-06 only 47,480 people did. Picture 11.1 shows how the number of Bachelors degrees in computer science has varied over time.

11.1.4   Who are they?

According to the Computer Research Association's Taulbee Survey, in 2007, approximately 88% of the people receiving a Bachelor's degree in computer science or computer engineering in North America were men, and 12% were women. 7% were international students, 15% were Asian American or Pacific Islanders, 5% were Hispanic, 4% were African American, and 66% were White.

The percent of women completing a Bachelor's degree in computer science peaked in 1984 at roughly 37%.

There are some schools with a much higher than average percentage of women students in computer science. For example, Carnegie Mellon University has roughly 40% women in its computer science major.

For more information on women in computer science, see:

- The Taulbee Survey:
  http://www.cra.org/statistics/

- The book: *Unlocking the Clubhouse: Women in Computing*, by J. Margolis and A. Fisher

11.1.5   What else do women study?

A great many women who select a computer science major do a minor or a double major in another subject. However, it's hard to get statistics on minors and double majors, so we can't give you any numbers.

You might consider majoring in computer science with a minor in another area, such as mathematics, writing, biomedical engineering, or art. Or you could combine a minor or double major in computer science with a major in another area of interest to you.

11.1.6   Why do women want to study computer science?

It turns out that very different things attract women and men to computer science. Women seem primarily interested in computers as *tools* to help other people or to do other types of work such as language translation. Men seem more interested in computers as objects in themselves.

Women who have decided to do a major in computer science cite as reasons:

- Enjoying computing

- The prospect of safe and secure employment

- The fact that they can take a CS major in different directions

- Encouragement by others

- The fact that CS is an exciting, changing field

- The fact that they can combine CS with other interests

These and other interesting statistics are contained in *Computing for a Purpose: Gender and Attachment to computer science*, by J. Margolis, A. Fisher, and F. Miller.

We hope that in this book we have shown you that computer science is enjoyable, that you can take your interest in computing in many different directions, and that computer science is an exciting, changing field. In the biographies in each chapter you have seen how women have combined interests in computer science with other interests, from music (Ada Lovelace) to children's education (Justine Cassell).

Think about which of the above reasons for doing a major in Computer Science most fits you.

11.1.7   Are there other majors I can take to become a computer scientist?

Yes. You can do a major in computer engineering, information technology, or information systems – even certain majors in cognitive science, business, or applied mathematics may work. However, if you want to be a computer scientist the simplest method is to do a computer science or software engineering major.

11.1.8   What courses are required to become a computer science major?

This depends on which college you go to. Most college computer science departments have a Web site that describes their courses in detail, sometimes even including the slides the professors use and the exams they give. For example, at Stony Brook the courses are described at
`http://www.cs.sunysb.edu/undergrad/cse_courses/index.html`.

A recommended curriculum for computer science programs is published by the Association for Computing Machinery (ACM). The topics it suggests are covered in many of the chapters in this book and include: programming languages, discrete mathematics, computer architecture, operating systems, databases, networks and security, theory of computation, data structures and algorithms, artificial intelligence, graphics and human-computer interaction, scientific computing, technical writing, and professional ethics. The curriculum is described at
`http://www.acm.org/education/curricula.html`.

Here are some things you should know, though.

- You **do not** have to take computer science in high school in order to be a computer science major.

- You **do not** have to know how to program a computer in order to be a computer science major.

- You **do not** have to be the world's greatest mathematician in order to be a computer science major.

- You **do not** have to have a computer at home in order to be a computer science major.

- You **do not** have to be a computer gamer in order to be a computer science major.

- Most importantly, you **do not** have to be a boy in order to be a computer science major!

11.1.9 Are there scholarships for computer science majors?

There are many scholarships for computer science majors, some of which are only for women. Many colleges and universities have merit-based (in addition to need-based) scholarships. Several government agencies fund scholarships for computer science majors. Also, many companies and organizations fund scholarships for computer science majors. Check out the Google scholarship for women, the Microsoft scholarship for women, the AAUW scholarship program, CRA W's scholarships for undergraduate research, and AT&T's scholarship program for women.

For more information on scholarships see:

- The Google Anita Borg scholarships:
  http://www.google.com/anitaborg/

- Microsoft scholarships:
  http://www.microsoft.com/college/ss_reqs.mspx

- The Barry M. Goldwater scholarship program:
  http://www.act.org/goldwater/index.html

- Lucent Technologies Summer Research Program:
  http://www.bell-labs.com/employment/srp/info.html

- Society of Women Engineers scholarships:
  http://www.swe.org/

- CRA-W Distributed Mentor Project:
  http://www.cra.org/Activities/craw/dmp/

- AT&T Labs Fellowship:
  http://www.research.att.com/academic/alfp.html

- Department of Homeland Security scholarships:
  http://www.orau.gov/dhsed/05ugrad.htm

- Merck-AAAS Undergraduate Science Research program:
  http://nt1-ehrweb.aaas.org/merck/

- AAAS Science and Technology Policy Fellowship programs:
  http://fellowships.aaas.org/02_Programs/02_Congress.shtml

11.1.10   Are there other ways to become a computer scientist?

If you are not college-minded, you can become an information technology (IT) professional by apprenticing yourself to a parent or friend who is an IT professional, by doing an associate's degree in computer science, or by acquiring *certifications*, such as Microsoft's MCSE (Microsoft Certified Systems Engineer) or Sun's Solaris certification.

The U.S. Department of Labor reports that 65.3% of computer programmers have at least a Bachelor's degree. A Bachelor's degree is expected more often of software engineers, systems analysts, database administrators, and computer scientists and less often of computer support specialists and systems administrators. With a degree you will generally find it easier to get a good job and to advance in your career.

11.1.11   What if I do a different undergraduate major and then want to become a computer scientist?

This is a very interesting question. Many of the faculty members in the Computer Science Department at Stony Brook do not have undergraduate majors in computer science. Their undergraduate majors include computer science, applied mathematics, mathematics, electrical engineering, physics, computer engineering, industrial engineering, fine arts and music. Reading the biographies in this book, you will notice that many of the profiled computer scientists did not do an undergraduate degree in computer science.

Obviously, if you have not yet started college and want to be a computer scientist, the easiest and safest major would be computer science (possibly with a second major or minor in another area of interest to you). However, with the appropriate mathematical and programming background, you can first get a Bachelor's degree in another subject, and then get a Master's degree in computer science.

11.1.12   Can I do a computer science major and still be pre-med?

Yes! Just be sure to take the appropriate physics, biology, and chemistry sequences. There is great need for people knowledgeable about computer science in medical informatics as well as other areas such as biomedical engineering, business and law.

11.1.13 After getting a Bachelor's degree in computer science, should I go on and get a Master's degree in computer science?

Some people continue on to get a Master's degree right after they get their Bachelor's degree. Others get a job in industry after getting their Bachelor's degree and then later go back and get a Master's degree, sometimes part time or at night, and often paid for by their employer. It takes one or two years if you go full time.

Getting a Master's degree increases your specialized knowledge in certain aspects of computer science. But more importantly, it increases your ability to learn new technology by yourself. As the field changes, you will spend a large amount of time learning new technology to stay current and advance in your career. That's one of the fun parts of the field, and getting a Master's degree is a big help.

We recommend getting a Master's degree if at all possible.

11.1.14 Should I get a Ph.D. degree in computer science?

Getting a Ph.D. degree takes an additional four to seven years after getting a Bachelor's degree. In most cases, while you are in a Ph.D. program, you are offered a part-time position as a Teaching Assistant or Research Assistant, which pays you a (barely) living wage and also pays your tuition. According to the Taulbee Survey, the median nine-month salary in 2007 for Teaching and Research Assistants was about $18,000-$19,000 in the best departments. Research Assistants usually got additional compensation for the three summer months.

When you are in a Ph.D. program, you select a subarea of computer science that is particularly exciting for you. First you learn all that is known about that subarea by taking courses, reading technical papers, and attending technical conferences. Then you perform research in that area, hopefully in a new and exciting way that will extend what is known about computers or what can be done with computers.

You will become an apprentice to a professor who is an expert in that area, and you will learn to do research under his or her supervision. As you get results, you will publish those results in technical journals and present them at national and international conferences, where you will meet many of the experts in that area and the other Ph.D. students doing research in that area. When you are done with the research, you will write a Ph.D. dissertation describing your research. You will then defend that dissertation in front of a panel of faculty members from your department and elsewhere. Then you will by awarded your Ph.D. degree.

After getting the Ph.D. degree, you can become a college professor or an industrial researcher. So if you are interested in become a professor and/or doing research in computer science, you should get a Ph.D.

11.2   Being a Computer Scientist

11.2.1   What jobs are open to a computer scientist?

As a computer scientist, you could work as: a system programmer, an applications programmer, a database administrator, an operations research specialist, a systems analyst, a technical sales representative, a technical support representative, a computer systems manager, a technical writer, a web developer, a game programmer, a high school teacher of computer science, a computer science researcher, a university professor of computer science, and on and on.

Think outside the box, too. Imagine:

- You could do graphical rendering for the next great animated feature film.

- You could be the Web page designer for a great nonprofit organization, such as Doctors Without Borders. You would be their first face to the world.

- You could design the next generation of language translation software, helping people who speak different languages communicate with each other.

- You could be the person who defines the next great encryption protocol.

- You could be a usability engineer, working to make the next generation of smart cars safer and more user friendly.

- You could write the program that finds the cure for cancer.

You could work for a software company such as Google or Microsoft, a hardware company such as IBM or Sun, or a non-CS company such as: a bank, accounting firm, stock broker, airline, hospital, insurance company, online service provider, consulting company, store, telecommunications company, utility company, or manufacturing company, and on and on. You could also work for the government, for example for the Defense Department, the Federal Bureau of Investigation, the Department of Homeland Security, or the Internal Revenue Service. Finally you could work for a university. Most jobs for computer scientists are in companies whose primary focus is not information technology.

11.2.2   How many jobs are there for computer scientists?

The College Board, the organization that administers the SAT examinations, has a Web site with a page, *10 Hottest Careers for College Graduates*, and on that page is a list of the "Occupations with the Most New

Jobs: Bachelor's Degrees." Four of these ten occupations are Computer-Science related: computer systems analyst; computer software engineer, applications; network systems and data communications analyst; and network and computer systems administrator. (Three of the other six are education jobs. The remaining three are accountant/auditor, securities and financial services sales agent, and construction manager.)

The U.S. Department of Labor agrees: while jobs for computer programmers will grow about as fast as average through 2012, other computer science-related jobs (software engineer, support specialist, system administrator, systems analyst, database administrator, computer scientist) will grow faster than average, and jobs for software engineers are projected to increase faster than almost any other occupation.

Similarly, the National Association of Colleges and Employers in its 2005 salary survey identified "Software Design and Development" as one of the top 10 jobs for students with new Bachelor's degrees, and the job with the highest starting salary among the top 10. Computer science majors with new Bachelor's degrees earn the second highest average starting salary overall. (We talk about salaries in Question 11.2.4.)

In 2006, Money magazine published a list of the 50 "Best Jobs in America." Number 1 on the list was software engineer, and number 7 was computer/IT analyst. Interestingly, number 2 on the list was college professor. One measure they used in making up this list was their "10 year job growth forecast." That forecast

- For software engineers is 46.07%

- For computer/IT analysts is 36.10%

- For college professors is 31.39%

According to the U.S. Department of Labor, women made up about 27% of people employed in computer and mathematical occupations in 2004. As the number of CS-related jobs grows, more women will be needed to fill the employment gap, and they will be paid accordingly.

For more information on computer science jobs, see:

- The College Board Web page
  http://www.collegeboard.com

- The Bureau of Labor Statistics' Occupational Outlook Handbook:
  http://stats.bls.gov/oco/oco1002.htm

- Job Web's salary and benefits page:
  http://www.jobweb.com/SalaryInfo/default.htm

11.2.3 Will my job be outsourced?

You might have been warned not to become a computer scientist because so many "IT jobs" are being outsourced to India and China. Is that a good reason to decide not to become a computer scientist?

First of all, the words "IT" (Information Technology) refer to many types of computer-related jobs other than computer scientist, for example a help desk person or a low-level programming job. And, indeed, many of these lower-level jobs are being outsourced to countries where people are willing to work for a much lower salary than would be required in this country. But yes, many high-level design and programming jobs are also being outsourced. And several companies have established research and development laboratories in such countries as India, China, England, Ireland, and Israel to perform research in various areas of computer science.

However, as we said in Question 11.2.2, even with the reality of outsourcing, computer-related jobs are still predicted to be among the fastest growing occupations over the next decade and beyond. The technology is changing so fast and the need for new computer professionals is growing so rapidly that there will be plenty of jobs for computer professionals in the United States as well as in all the other countries of the world. In fact, in 2004 Bill Gates predicted that there would be a serious shortage of computer professionals in the United States by the year 2012.

Outsourcing is not the real issue. The issue is what country will be the world leader in conceiving and developing the coming generations of exciting new applications of computers and in starting the new companies that will produce and sell those applications.

Instead of using outsourcing as a reason not to become a computer scientist, we should instead view it as a challenge. These other countries are challenging our technical leadership in the computer area. That leadership has been an important factor in our economic growth and well-being over the past several decades. For example, companies such as Google, Microsoft, eBay, Cisco, and Dell were formed by American entrepreneurs, many of them while they were still in college.

Do we want to retain that leadership? If so, we need to attract more, not fewer computer scientists who will develop the new concepts, technologies, and products that will certainly be developed elsewhere if not here. For example, the Chinese language translator for an earring computer will be developed somewhere. Do we want it developed here?

If the word "outsourcing" scares off too many young people, and not enough smart, creative, entrepreneurial people in the United States decide to become computer scientists, we might find ourselves giving up our leadership to India, China, or some other country. You are the generation that will determine whether or not we retain our position as leaders in computer technology. And women have an important role to play in meeting that challenge, not only because you comprise (at least) half of the creative and smart people in the country, but also, as we have said, because you bring a unique perspective to the field.

Field	Starting Salary
engineering	$49,636
computer science	$49,110
business	$41,233
health sciences	$39,499
sciences	$38,121
communications	$31,900
humanities, social sciences	$31,212
education	$30,646

Table 11.1: Starting salaries in a variety of fields.

11.2.4 How much does a computer scientist make?

According to Payscale.com, which collects advertised starting salaries, the median starting salaries in 2008 for someone with a Bachelor's degree in computer science were about:

- $57,000 for a software engineer or programmer

- $40,000 for a web developer

- $60,000 for a database administrator

- $49,000 for a network administrator

- $45,000 for a computer programmer/analyst

If you want to compare the starting salaries of computer scientists with those of people with Bachelor's degrees in other fields, Table 11.1 shows the average starting salaries offered to people with a Bachelor's degree in 2005 in a variety of fields, according to the National Association of Colleges and Employers salary survey.

If you go on and get a Ph.D. degree, you might then become a college professor or an industrial researcher. You might start out as a post-doc – a temporary postdoctoral research position at a university. According to a Taulbee survey on academic salaries, the median nine month salaries for computer science post-docs and professors in 2006 were

- $80,255 for a new Ph.D. hired as a Post-doc.

- $82,781 for a new Ph.D. hired as an Assistant Professor

- $120,521 for a Full Professor

Note that most faculty members have research grants, which pay additional salary for the three summer months that their nine months (academic year) salaries do not include. In addition many faculty members have the opportunity to do outside consulting that can produce additional income.

According to a (different) Taulbee survey on industrial researcher salaries, the median compensation (salary plus bonuses) for Ph.D. researchers at industrial research laboratories in 2004 were

- $108,771 for a new Ph.D.

- $158,644 after 16 years

According to the 2006 Money magazine article on the 50 Best Jobs in America, the average pay (salary plus bonus)

- For software engineers, is $80,427

- For computer/IT analysts is $83,427

- For college professors is $81,491

Women in general make less money than men. The weekly median salary of women age 16 and over (averaged over a large number of occupations) is 79% that of men age 16 and over, according to data provided by the Commission on Professionals in Science and Technology. The "wage gap" for women in CS-related jobs is somewhat smaller. The weekly median salary of women in computer and mathematical occupations is 80.2% that of men, and the weekly median salary for women who are computer and information systems managers is 89% that of men.

For more information on salaries, see:

- Payscale.com:
  http://www.payscale.com/salary-survey/vid-65728/fid-6886

- National Association of Colleges and Employers
  http://www.naceweb.org/salarysurvey/salary_survey.asp

- Taulbee survey on academic salaries
  http://www.cra.org/statistics/

- Taulbee survey on industrial salaries
  http://www.cra.org/CRN/articles/nov05/waters.html

- Commission on Professionals in Science in Technology:
  http://www.cpst.org/STEM_Group5.cfm

11.2.5   What does a computer scientist do at work?

The answer to that question depends on the particular job the computer scientist has. Answering the questions in Picture 11.2 can help you figure out what kind of computer science job you would like to have.

What Do You Want to Do?

What would you like to wear to work?
a) pajamas; b) jeans and a t-shirt; c) business casual; d) dressy suits

For whom would you like to work?
a) a big company; b) a small company; c) a start-up company; d) a school; e) myself

Where would you like to work?
a) Wall Street; b) Main Street; c) My street

When would you like to work?
a) 9-5; b) all the time; c) when I choose

With whom would you like to work?
a) other computer scientists; b) co-workers who are not computer scientists; c) students; d) customers/clients; e) no one!

Do you want to:
a) make a difference in the world; b) help other people; c) make lots of money; d) be respected

Figure 11.2: What do you want to do?

No matter how you answered those questions, there are computer science jobs that satisfy those conditions. That's one of the really nice things about computer science.

Almost no computer scientist spends all of the working day programming alone (unless he or she works from home as, for example, a technical writer or Web developer). Technical support personnel answer calls and go out to fix problems. Software engineers, in addition to programming, attend meetings, perform design and testing tasks with their co-workers, and these days might even program in groups. Systems analysts travel often, meeting with customers to define the application to be developed. College professors interact with students, other faculty members, and their technical colleagues throughout the world.

As an illustration, the cousin, the husband, and the brother of Amanda, who are software engineers or systems engineers, were asked how they spend their days. They said they spend over half of their time interacting with other people, either to help them or to plan activities with them.

So what do Amanda and Phil do all day as computer science professors (in addition to writing this book)? We teach courses; advise students; do research; participate in the activities of the Computer Science Department (attend faculty meetings, serve on committees, etc); and participate in the activities of the national and international computer science community (review papers for journals and conferences, serve on committees for professional organizations etc.).

Before Phil came to Stony Brook, he was a researcher at the research laboratory of a large multinational company. What did he do all day? He did research; participated in the activities of the laboratory and company (served on laboratory and company committees and task forces, etc.); and participated in the activities of the national and international computer science community (as above).

11.2.6   Can I be involved in a start-up company and get rich?

Since technology is changing so rapidly, there is always the opportunity to discover an exciting new use of that technology and start a company to market that new use. You can do this after getting a Ph.D., a Master's, a Bachelor's, or even with no degree at all. There are many sources of money to help.

Five Stony Brook computer science professors have started new companies, two of which have been very successful. Recently some of Phil's students in his undergraduate Software Engineering class developed some new software to schedule doctors, residents, and nurses in a hospital and started a new company to market that software. With hard work and help, they got about $200,000 in startup money to pay for costs and salaries.

Starting a new business takes a certain entrepreneurial spirit and the intensity to stay up all night to develop the required software. Many women have been involved in startups. Remember that Sandy Lerner was one of the founders of Cisco Systems.

11.2.7   How does a computer scientist stay up-to-date?

It is particularly important for computer scientists to stay up-to-date because the field is changing so rapidly. And the field will continue to change rapidly throughout your entire career. In fact that is one of the most fun parts of working in computer science.

As an example, when Phil started his professional career, there were no commercial computers (or computer science departments). His Bachelor's degree was in electrical engineering, where he learned to design electronic systems using vacuum tubes. All of that knowledge became obsolete within ten years when transistors replaced vacuum tubes. He has spent his whole career learning all the new technology that has developed over the years. He tells his students that it's been fun.

Many computer scientists stay up-to-date by taking ongoing training courses, for example certifications, for which their employers might pay. Many belong to professional societies such as the Association for Computing Machinery, and as a result get articles and other materials that help them stay current. Many go to technical conferences, where they take tutorials on new areas, hear presentations of the latest ideas, and talk to other professionals. Many buy textbooks and other books that cover the new technologies. Finally, computer scientists are notorious gossips, always showing each other the latest exciting thing.

For more information on keeping up to date, check out:

- The ACM:
  http://www.acm.org

- InformationWeek:
  http://www.informationweek.com

- Wired:
  http://www.wired.com

11.2.8   What if I want to get married?

The two-body problem refers to the situation where you are married, and both you and your husband need to find jobs that will advance your careers and are reasonably close to each other.

That can indeed be a difficult problem no matter what field you are in, but increasingly employers understand the problem and are willing to help a spouse of a prospective employee find an appropriate job.

Nevertheless this is a topic that you should certainly discuss with your future husband (when you get to that stage in your life).

A very interesting book that is devoted to this topic is *Kidding Ourselves: Breadwinning, Babies, and Bargaining Power*, by Rhona Mahoney, Basic Books 1996.

11.2.9   What if I want to have a family?

It is no harder to balance family and career for a computer scientist than for a business person, engineer, lawyer, or doctor. In fact, because in some cases a computer scientist can work from home, it may be a little easier.

However, if you take time off to have a family you will have to stay current. You can do this by participating in a professional society, taking online training courses, or beefing up your certifications when you rejoin the work force.

11.2.10   Isn't it lonely being a women in computer science?

It can be lonely to be in the minority in any group. But remember we said that more than 25% of the people working in computer-related jobs are women. So, no matter where you work (or go to school), you probably will be able to find a number of women about your age who you can socialize with and a smaller number of older women who can act as mentors and guides. The culture among women in computing is very supportive.

You can also find a support network to give you a sense of belonging. For example, check out the Systers network at http://www.systers.org.

Remember, there is nothing lonelier than being in the happiest group of people, but being unhappy yourself, as you would be if you chose a career simply because it was 'easy' or 'had a lot of women in it.'

You might feel as you look at careers that the 'easy' path would be to become a nurse, or teacher, or to study psychology, or history, or business. Your friends, your parents, and society at large (especially certain magazines, including computer science-related magazines!) might imply or say that computer science is not a good career, or not a good career for a woman. You might look at some of the statistics in this chapter and think that the low numbers of women in computer science mean that you should not become a computer scientist.

We encourage you to see things a little differently. Think about what *you* want to do. What kind of person are you? What makes you excited? Don't see the small number of women in computer science as a disadvantage. See it as an opportunity: to make an impact, to make a difference, to stand out from the crowd. As Robert Frost said,

Two roads diverged in a wood, and I –
I took the one less traveled by,
And that has made all the difference.

11.2.11 Will I be treated with respect as a woman in computer science?

Will I be treated with respect as a woman when I am in college and later when I have a job? Will I be teased or taunted? Will I get the raises or promotions I deserve? Will I be sexually harassed? Will I feel comfortable?

Unfortunately, all of these bad things can happen no matter what kind of career you select. For example you might think that nursing and teaching are both woman-friendly professions, but

- In a 2004 Canadian study, 76% of nurses reported that they had been sexually harassed at some time in their career.

- According to a survey made by the Rand Organization in the year 2000, while 63% of the high school teachers in the state of North Carolina were women, only 24% of the high school principals were women. Based on these numbers, it's hard to believe that women and men teachers are given equal opportunities to be promoted to become principals.

These examples are interesting (and a bit discouraging), but they don't answer the question of how you can expect to be treated in computer science.

Amanda's experience is that women are increasingly accepted as computer scientists. This is particularly true in companies – younger companies, like Google, or older ones that have a track record of being good places for women to work. She also thinks that what you want to do with your life, and your confidence in yourself, matter more than what anyone else thinks about you. If computer science makes you excited more than anything else, then you should do it.

When you are looking for a job at a company, do a little bit of research. Figure out how many of staff and managers are women. Try to find information about benefits, for example, does the company offer paid maternity leave? See if you can find the company on a list of 100 best places to work (some magazines to check out: Fortune, Working Mother, ComputerWorld).

11.3   What Does a Computer Scientist Do in Her Spare Time?

11.3.1   Is it true that all computer scientists are geeks?

No! Computer scientists love their work, but they also do many other activities. We know computer scientists who: play tennis, basketball and ice hockey; run and ride in marathons; play instruments in orchestras; are artists; build houses for Habitat for Humanity; write books about religion; travel all over the world; blow glass; build and donate computers to nonprofits; take photographs for gourmet cooking societies; participate in the Mars Society (dedicated to sending humans to Mars); take ballroom dancing lessons; are Goths; play in rock bands; write science fiction; and race cars.

Computer scientists can take their job as their life and make a glamorous, well-traveled, exciting life out of it. Or they can take it as their job and have successful, happy leisure lives that have nothing to do with technology. Or they can be somewhere in between.

11.3.2   What are some professional societies or clubs a computer scientist might join?

The Association for Computing Machinery, or ACM, is the primary society a computer scientist would join. It has special interest groups (or SIGs) on computer-human interaction, operating systems, databases, computer science education, and many other topics. It has an electronic library, magazines, conferences, local chapters, a job/career center and online training courses.

One society that women computer scientists can join is the Systers list, an international mailing list of over 20,000 women in information technology all around the world.

Here are the Web pages of some CS-related societies:

- The ACM: http://www.acm.org

- The CRA: http://www.cra.org

- The IEEE: http://www.ieee.org

- The Society of Women Engineers: http://www.swe.org/

- The Society of Professional Hispanic Engineers: http://www.shpe.org/

- The Systers List: http://www.systers.org

11.4 The Bottom Line

The bottom line is this:

- Computer science degrees are interesting and challenging.

- Computer science jobs are plentiful, exciting, and well-paid.

- A career in computer science can be challenging, rewarding, and an opportunity to make an important contribution to society.

- Our country needs more computer scientists.

- Women have a unique contribution to make to computer science.

- You can be a computer scientist.

Come join us!